Introduction

WHAT IF I WERE TO TELL YOU that we all live in a different version of the movie *The Matrix*? If you haven't seen it, the movie asks the question: What would happen if we were born into a completely immersive virtual reality simulation that is complete with all the sights, sounds, smells, tastes, and touches of reality, but is not reality? To make it seem even more real, what if, just like in the movie, everyone experiencing the Matrix is immersed in it from the moment they are born?

In that movie, the hero finds a way to recognize and get free of the control of the Matrix. What if each of us was the unrealized hero of that story, but we have fallen asleep into a forgetful dream of believing, fully mistaking that dream for reality? How could anyone tell the difference between actual reality and the Matrix if we were born into it?

Just like the oracle in that movie, what if all that I—or anyone—can do for you is give you a chance to remember what we've each been taught to forget?

What if I promised you that magic is real and emotional suffering and death are illusions? What if I could show you that the keys to freedom from all mental and emotional suffering are already hidden inside each problem, and that each time we feel the pain of that problem it is a message from an oracle, trying to wake us up to the memory of who we truly are?

What if, in fact, the reality is that we are all in a mythological battle that we are completely unaware of, but that will literally determine the fate of the world?

In virtually all myths there's a reluctant hero who, faced with a life-or-death challenge, goes in search of a savior, only to realize in the end that s/he is the one; that the ability to overcome the challenge is within, and that s/he must rise up and face it.

Our lives are shaped and guided by stories and emotions. The stories we are told become the stories that we tell. The more we hear them, the more we believe them. Words and emotions have power. When used as tools, they help us to better understand who we are, where we come from, and where we are going; but when used as weapons, they can do immense harm.

There are only two paths: the path of our limited individual perspectives and the path of reality.

Like in the movie *The Matrix*, our personal perspectives are what we believe to be true, but which, left unexamined, can lead us down a path that we believe is the right direction but is only a path of suffering and confusion. One path leads us on a journey to awaken to the truth of ourselves and the world—the truth that sets us free. The other leads us astray, taking us deeper and deeper into a false reality based solely on the limited information from our personal perspectives, while promising to lead to a freedom that never comes. The problem is that we were all taught to follow the wrong path from the very moment we were born.

I never expected how unexpected my life has been. If anyone had told me at the beginning, I would not have believed them. I would never have believed that everything I had been taught in my childhood, by everyone around me—my family, my friends, my teachers, and society—was wrong.

I would never have imagined that I would wake up blind just after graduating from college. I would never have believed the amount of mental and emotional suffering that followed. Given all the pain and confusion, I would never have thought that I would find my way out at all, let alone experience the strange twist of fate that changed everything for me.

Most surprising of all, I never would have believed that it was all for my benefit—that life was happening for me and not to me. I never would have believed any of it until I directly experienced it for myself.

Let me start by saying that I am sorry. I have already failed you. I can never give you the direct experiences that my life has given to me—all the pain and confusion, the struggles and the heartache, the life-changing realizations. Not only is it impossible to share these with you, but I would spare you that pain. I would never want anyone to face the suffering and confusion that I faced without also experiencing the unexpected possibilities that I have uncovered.

I want to tell you about my unexpected journey so that you might also have the breakthroughs that I had. Looking back on the journey I have lived and the discoveries I have made, I see that it was worth all the suffering. My journey began with tremendous pain and confusion.

I thought that if I could outlast my profoundly confusing and isolated childhood, my better life would start when I got to college. I wouldn't find out until I went to college that things don't turn out the way we want them to, no matter how much we wish they did. You have probably heard the truism "Man plans, God laughs," right?

I went from graduating from college with honors and a solid future ahead of me to feeling like a discarded blind person. I suffered from debilitating panic and anxiety attacks, as well as depression and health issues. All my life plans were gone forever in a single night. What came after was struggling with months of depression, passing out from anxiety attacks, and distracting myself with food, which only created more problems.

I had no understanding at the time, but all of it was a gift. All of life is a gift. It's only now that I have come out of the other side of the storm that I can offer up what I have learned. I can offer and share the map I made along my journey.

Mine was a journey out of suffering and into deeper understanding. I learned so many things that seemed like suffering at first but actually held the keys that ended my suffering. It's only after learning the lessons offered that I finally understand that this very process is how to grow stronger and more resilient.

Life wasn't punishing me; it was just showing me over and over how things work. The problem was that I was taught completely differently and kept refusing to accept it. Until I learned the lessons offered by my struggles, they would cycle until I did. I couldn't start my journey at the destination. I would have to figure it out along the way.

I made the mistakes I was taught to make. I learned to believe all the misunderstandings of those around me. I never questioned the world around me; I had just been trying to survive, to outlast the pain, hoping that somehow it would end. I didn't know there was any other way to live. I had no idea that, until I questioned the one assumption at the root of all my problems, I would not find any solutions.

I would have to lose my sight to learn to see. I would have to be poor to find real prosperity. I would have to suffer deeply to realize one single thing: To be free, I would have to take the false premise that I had been taught and make it true. Somehow, I would have to make the dysfunction in my life and the world become function.

The dysfunction taught to me from the very moment I was born was twofold: a lie of the heart and a lie of the mind. I was taught that my personal set of beliefs was the truth that could set me free, and that by listening to the thoughts generated by fear and anger and following their advice, negative emotions can lead to positive outcomes.

Albert Einstein said that the definition of insanity is doing the same thing over and over and expecting a different outcome, and yet this is what we are all taught that we must do. We must satisfy the requirements of everyone around us, as well as our own, to make them and ourselves happy. Only then can we find love and happiness. But what if this is a false premise? A faulty assumption that has never been examined? An impossible requirement that only leads to insanity? And yet we are all taught that it is the only way to freedom.

Through my experiences, I have learned that there is another way. The way that Einstein pointed to when he said that you can never solve any problem from the same level that creates it. A way through which an insane world makes complete sense. An objective perspective that requires no opinions. No facts or figures, definitions or knowledge. A place beyond belief that is true-hearted and genuine.

These are what I have come to call the two paths. They are the path that I was taught in childhood—the path of conditional love and negative emotionality—and the path that I would have to discover through confusion and struggle. The reunification of heart and mind. The path of love and the functional dynamics of objective truth.

REVIEWS FROM AMAZON...

"A most interesting book. As a guy who reads lots of different genres of books, I can honestly say that this particular one opened my eyes to new and different ways to deal with life's supreme challenges as the author certainly has. Steven's personal experiences and challenges have far surpassed anything most of us have ever faced, and his approaches to addressing them have been unique, interesting and, most importantly, effective. A must-read!"

— Charles W. Faure

"A Unique Blend of Humor and Depth. The eloquent expression of The Two Paths *leaves a lasting impression, evoking a profound impact. I enthusiastically recommend it for its ability to create a shift in perspective. The material is presented with a remarkable depth that makes it easily digestible. The author's compelling stories, coupled with his personal realizations, stirred deep emotions and insights within me. This is a Must-Read!!"*

— Salima Sidiqi

"Interesting, raw, insightful read into the author's life experiences. The Two Paths *is an interesting read where the author is real, honest, and open about his life experiences. He uses humor and realness to express how he has used negative experiences, learned from them, and moved past the past to live a happier life with a more positive outlook on the future."*

— Susan S.

"The quickest I've ever finished a book, Great Read! ...What I appreciated most about The Two Paths *was its accessibility. Steve has a gift for presenting complex ideas without the burden of complicated jargon, making the book approachable even for those new to contemplating the nature of reality. While I'm certain each reader will find aspects of the book that resonate with them personally, for me, it often felt as though I was reading about my own life. Steve's narrative was not only easy to follow but also deeply engaging, ensuring that readers can explore profound concepts without feeling overwhelmed."*

— Mark Nisbett

"Excellent book, well worth reading! They say that life is an education, well this author has been to the school of hard knocks when it comes to the cards he's been dealt and instead of downing tools and taking one path, he's opted to face the challenges of another, garnering big truths along the way. This book is positively engaging. A serious subject delivered with personality and relatable content. The material beckons us to consider a different world for all, if only we can live this life from a love based perspective. On this path, all is possible…The Two Paths *calls us to question the imposed belief system that is drip-fed to us all from the moment we are born and to consider the author's findings as we seek the world beyond our limiting beliefs. This is a thoroughly engaging and enjoyable read with a truly inspirational tone…Everyone should read this book. Loved it!"

— *Fiona*

"Life altering yet easy and funny to read! The world is a rough place to live, and it seems to be getting worse everyday. Nothing seems to make sense anymore.

I was so surprised when I read this book at how easy it was to read, and funny, but really gave simple yet deeply profound understanding of it all. I'm not used to a book that is so actually deeply helpful to be a such easy read!

It has amazing perspectives on things and very practical ways to help us have a much happier life, despite all the negative chaos that swirls around us. It shows us how how not to be so affected and injured by the terrible struggles of life today in very easy to grasp ways…"

— *Shelly Kearns*

"I needed to read this book more than words can express. I felt called… in a way that went deeper than even my own understanding. …[E]ach word, each sentence, and each chapter was simply absorbed. My true self, the one that only observes and connects, was present, and because of that, I was able to completely transform my life.

…At times, I'd put the book down, and something would happen in my life. When I picked it back up, it was like an oracle, holding the exact answer I needed. The book is well-written, easy to digest, transformational, and essential. …I keep quoting analogies and passages from this book to my friends and anyone who will listen. This is the best book I've ever read. I didn't know who Steven Fidler was when I reluctantly bought this book, but now I can say that he has changed my life and added a deep knowing of, "We are all connected, and life is magic," to it because of The Two Paths. Sending all the love to anyone that is reading this."

— *Amazon Customer*

"Outstanding! A wonderful insight to expanding one's life!"

— *User F*

"Excellent read and very thought provoking. While there are several anec-dotes in the book which are in equal parts funny and thought provoking, I felt that the core message was very elegantly simple which in my book is a sign of great writing. The consistency and clarity of thought that the author is trying to present was refreshing and I have found myself often thinking about the ideas in here and applying them to situations in my own life, which is a great success for this book. The author comes across as a fantastic individual and a great human being too which is an added bonus. Highly recommend picking this one up!

— *Amazon Customer*

"Well worth the read!…I found myself stopping and taking the time to let the words sink in. At times I found myself thinking back on some of my own childhood experiences and re-thinking their impact based on Steven's perspective. Instead of remaining tied to perceived realities forged from painful and traumatic experiences earlier in his life, he shares with us his journey. He takes us on a quest and shows us how his curiosity to search for truth and deeper meaning, changed the way he lived and chooses to embrace life in all its fullness with a joyful heart.

In addition to his humor that shines through, I particularly liked the highlighted nuggets of insight peppered throughout the book taken from a variety of cultural, philosophical and religious sources and traditions. Whether you breeze through Steven's book or take the time to savor the wisdom in his words, it is definitely worth the read!"

— *Kindle User*

"A refreshingly accessible and deeply meaningful book…"

— *Amazon Customer*

The Two Paths

The Two Paths
Finding the World Beyond Belief

second edition

STEVEN FIDLER

Two Paths Publishing
Middlebury, Vermont

The Two Paths
Finding the World Beyond Belief, second edition

For more information about this book or the author, visit www.StevenFidler.net.

ISBN: 979-8-9880398-3-9
eISBN: 979-8-9880398-4-6
AUDIOBOOK: 979-8-9880398-5-3
Library of Congress Control Number: 2025920979

First edition 2023

Printed in the United States of America

Two Paths Publishing
www.StevenFidler.net

Disclaimer: This is a work of creative non-fiction. Unless otherwise indicated, all the names, characters, businesses, places, events and incidents in this book are either the product of the author's imagination or used in a poetic manner. Any resemblance to actual persons, living or dead, or actual events is purely coincidental.

Design and Layout updated from Andrea Leigh Ptak by Gotham City Graphics
Copyedited by Louise Watson
Cover Illustration by Mark Nisbett and Fiona O'Brien
Back Cover Photo by Nancy Merolle

DEDICATION

This book is dedicated to the unexpected journey and to all those amazing people we meet along the way. From my family to my favorite person to my truest friends, to my unexpected teachers, to all people everywhere.

This book is dedicated to all of us. We are all on this journey together. There is not one person in my life who hasn't been touched by people I will never meet, and yet they shaped the people we all know and love. Life is a never-ending web of invisible connections that touches us all.

TABLE OF CONTENTS

Introduction ix

Chapter 1   THE BIRTH OF CONFUSION, DELUSION, ... 1
            BORN INTO THE ILLUSION
            ACT ONE: THE FALL

Chapter 2   GROWING UP IN THE MATRIX 17
            ACT TWO: TRYING TO MAKE THE
            ROOTS OF DYSFUNCTION FUNCTION

Chapter 3   THE FUNCTION OF DYSFUNCTION:.................... 41
            UNKNOWINGLY FEEDING THE WRONG WOLF

Chapter 4   THE GOLDEN RULE: UNIVERSAL FUNCTION 61
            VERSUS INDIVIDUAL BELIEF
            ACT THREE: THE TRANSITION TO
            THE PATH OF REALITY

Chapter 5   TAKING BACK THE JOURNEY 79
            ACT FOUR: ALIGNING WITH REALITY

Chapter 6   THE ONE PROBLEM IN THE WORLD 109
            AND THE ONE SOLUTION

Chapter 7   ALL OF LIFE IS A GIFT:.................................... 141
            WE MUST ACTUALLY LIVE IT

Acknowledgments 157

About the Author 161

The Birth of Confusion, Delusion, Born into the Illusion
Act One: The Fall

If we never fall down, how could we
learn how to get back up again?
—Anonymous

THERE IS A BEAUTIFUL AND POWERFUL MOMENT in the movie *The Matrix*. In an early scene, Morpheus, the leader of the resistance, tells us what the Matrix is. He says that it is all around us. It can be seen when you look out your window or when you are watching television. You can feel it when you go to work or church and when you pay your taxes. He ends his explanation by saying that the Matrix is the world that has been pulled over your eyes to blind you to the truth. What if the Matrix is not just a movie? What if that is true for every one of us? What would that look like if it is true? Let's find out.

I was born into a lower middle class working family. We weren't poor, but we certainly weren't secure by any means. My dad was a steel worker then, and my mother was a stay-at-home mom. We were the stereotypical nuclear family. I had one older brother, and of course we had Thumper, the family dog. We also had what everyone struggles with. We had problems.

It's amazing what defines us when we are young. We have literally zero ability to take care of ourselves, from our food, clothing, and shelter to our choices of what to believe and what we are allowed to do. Childhood is, for at least a good few years, a time when we cannot choose in any way—an experiment in confusion and adaptation.

There are good and bad times, but the things that really stay with us are the high-impact things, both good and bad, that hit us right in the feels. Things that touch our hearts as well as things that scar. My childhood experience was my baseline, my norm. I realize now that there is no norm. Those things that happen along the way, based on which we draw our conclusions and create our perspectives, are unique to each person, just like our DNA. The only difference is that, as children, we don't realize the impact that events—and our conclusions about them—are having on our long-term life perspectives. Especially the traumatic things. When you are a kid, it is unavoidable. We all fall into confusion.

I remember the first time I felt deeply violated. I was around the standard age when I was ready to go from diapers to big-boy pants. My mom was getting a little impatient and didn't know how to speed up the transition, so she did what people do: She asked someone else.

She had taken the dog to the vet and, while there, asked the veterinarian's assistant for advice about how to get me from diapers to full-time potty. She didn't know the woman or put any real thought into her response. My mom just heard the answer and decided to give it a try.

The woman had told her to do with me what they do with dogs to potty train them: The next time I filled up a diaper, she should push my face down toward it and shout, "BAD! BAD!" That is exactly what she did. We really don't realize the impact our thoughts, words, and actions have on ourselves and others.

We were at my grandmother's house. I must have had a good breakfast, because I really filled that diaper. I remember the sense of confusion. Why was I being stripped down and why was my loaded, reeking diaper being put onto the floor? Why was my mom forcefully putting me on my hands and knees and pushing my head down toward that full diaper while yelling "BAD!" over and over? Why was she doing this in front of my brother, who laughed and cheered her on? It was the first time confusion, fear, and humiliation overwhelmed my senses. I felt myself disassociate. I felt my mind shut down while my body resisted.

Looking back on it now, I know that because my mom took a complete stranger's advice, this and other childhood events were totally unfair. There was no way I wouldn't feel confused when I was a child. It's physiologically guaranteed. The brain takes seven years to develop the physiological structures of a fully functioning mental capacity, before there is any chance to even begin to learn how to process things and understand. During those seven years, the brain and nervous system are also forming neurological patterns that we are all completely unaware of.

We don't have a concept of words, let alone language, until about age 4, and thoughts are made of words, so it's not like I could go back to it afterwards and think about it. There is nothing that I could have done to change any of the bizarre, confusing, and scary things that happened to me.

We are all subject to this thing called neuroplasticity. Neuroplasticity is how we form habitual thought patterns. It's a creation of connections that form habits. A hardwiring of stimulus and response that we are completely unaware of. As a child, I had no idea that with everything I was being told and every emotion I was investing in, my beliefs were being hard-wired into my physical neurology.

That is seven years of misunderstanding, guaranteed. Seven years of forming habits and neurology that become the foundations of our personal perspectives. The worst part is that neuroplasticity and habit creation go in both directions. I only ever heard that practice makes perfect. No one ever told me that practice makes imperfect as well.

Given my lack of understanding and physiological brain development, this bizarre event was incomprehensible to me. I had seen my family raise the family dog this way. I concluded that I was no longer a part of the family proper; I was like the family dog. I backed away and lost trust in ways that I couldn't realize at that age. I just knew that something was different and something I'd had before, some sense of trust or family, or maybe even just knowing where I fit in the world, was gone.

To my mom and brother, however, it meant nothing. My mom was just trying out what someone had recommended, and my brother thought it was hilarious. For them, life simply returned to the household norm. But for me, things were never the same. I learned that childhood was a list of requirements to be met before anyone would love me. This was being hard-wired into my very neurology and informing the beliefs that made up my perspective on who I was and how the world worked.

Thousands of experiences filled up those first seven years, when all of those around me were defining me and I lacked the cognitive ability to question or understand their labels and definitions, the punishments and rewards. Seven years of conditional love: withholding love when I did what they didn't like, and rewarding me when they approved, after I conformed.

When I was around the age of 6, more confusing and traumatic things came along. My dad drank. Just beer, like everyone else's father that I knew. He worked hard and to this day, he is a playful and generous person. I learned so many good things from him. It didn't happen often, but when he drank too much, it created some truly memorable and scary times.

He was raised by a father who gambled at the racetrack. Horse racing was his thing. You see, my dad didn't know how to be a dad; he was raised to believe that a good father was measured by how well he could provide financially for the family. His own father was not able to provide well, and my dad grew up in significant poverty. His father was emotionally unavailable as well.

We can only do as well as we know, so my dad did the best with what he knew. He took us down to the racetrack as a family. He tried to make it a family thing. The racetrack isn't designed with family in mind. Back then, it stank of stale beer and cigar smoke. I noticed that there were no other kids or families there. The patrons were nearly all men. There was a smattering of girlfriends and wives, but there was a seedy feel to it that I didn't like. It scared me. The people all seemed sad and hopeful to me. Not the good kind of hope, but the kind of hope you have when you are sick and you hope the suffering ends.

My dad really enjoyed it, though, and I wanted to make my dad happy. As the evening wore on, he drank his standard two or three beers. I personally think that they spiked the beer at the track to get a bit more of an advantage. I am not sure if that was the case, or if my dad just lost himself in the rush of enjoyment he found at the races, but he got so drunk that he was seeing double by the time the last race was over.

The racetrack was about an hour and a half from the house and we had to drive home. When my dad got drunk, it always scared me. He acted like a totally different person. We had a long trip home, and he wouldn't let my mom drive.

I was sitting behind him in the passenger seat while he drove. He was holding one hand over one eye while he was driving and seeing double. I watched over his shoulder as we were weaving back and forth, into and out of the headlights of the oncoming traffic. I was terrified. With every hard swerve back into our lane, with every time my mom exclaimed "JIM!" to alert him that we were drifting dangerously close to the wrong lane, I was sure I was going to die.

As each oncoming car passed by, I squeezed my eyes shut. I didn't want to see the car that might finally be the one that we would hit. My stomach clenched in knots, I dug my hands into the back of my dad's seat and clung on for dear life. I could only relax when we finally made it home and parked in our driveway.

We really are totally reliant on our parents for survival as children. They try to provide all our physical and emotional needs—our food, shelter, and clothing, as well as the money to keep the furnace on in the winter.

The way we view ourselves and the world is also incredibly impacted by how much they show us their love for us, as well as what they believe. They are like gods to us when we are children. We are totally vulnerable to their decisions, both good and bad. We are vulnerable to their emotions, both good and bad. The only thing is that we don't realize that they don't really have things figured out either. We can't relate to them as emotionally struggling, like we are as children. We don't realize that like us, they have, or had, hopes and dreams—or even that they were once children themselves, with their own childhood pains and confusions.

In truth, there is very little difference between our emotional struggles as children and their emotional struggles as adults. All of these circumstances are the reason for the saying in psychological circles, "Seven years of childhood, a lifetime of therapy."

My dad's drinking reared its head in lots of ways while I was growing up. He moved from working at the steel mill to selling real estate, where he met with great success. It's a very true statement that you can change your circumstances all you like, but your problems—until you learn their lessons—follow you.

He worked a lot and he was really good at his work. He started making better money and became a really good provider. He also began to use work as an excuse to hide from the part that he wasn't good at: being a father.

I remember the nights when he wouldn't come home immediately after work. That handful of times when he didn't call or let anyone know where he was or if he was okay. During those times, he was drinking or at the racetrack. He would come home after midnight. Sometimes after the bars had closed or the last race finished at the track. No matter how late it got before he finally came home, I couldn't sleep. I worried about him the whole time.

One night he came home drunk and went straight to his bedroom and, without saying anything, began to pack a suitcase. I remember whispering to my mom about hiding his keys. I remember trying to distract him while my mom and I played the sad new game of "hide the keys." We all tried to understand what was going on while he was packing, and it left me with the fear that my family could fall apart at any moment.

There was no obvious event or trigger that would send my dad into a drinking binge. I wasn't aware of any signs of a bad morning or any arguments that precipitated them. His binges didn't happen often, and that made them even harder. That unpredictability impacted me. I lost a sense of certainty that we would stay together as a family. There was no way to earn it or predict it. It was a constant unknown, as well as a guarantee that could never be prepared for.

Yes, my parents loved me, but yes, my parents had their own pains, and as a child I had no ability mentally or emotionally to understand. I came to my own conclusions without any real understanding, and they were all rooted in fear. Later I would grow to be a teenager, and when I got stronger, I got angry.

THE PERSPECTIVE PARADIGM PROBLEM

We are all brought up with variations on these themes. In some way, we all get confused and we all suffer. That is where we all begin. This created my first obstacle in understanding myself and the world. I had mistaken my perspective for reality.

Due to the potty training incident, I concluded that I was less. Not an important member of the family, but more like the family dog. As a result of this conclusion, I stayed out of the way and faded into the background. Given my dad's instability, his drinking and his erratic and destabilizing behaviors, I made the decision to hide my emotional needs from my parents. I was too afraid to ask for anything and the conditional love hurt too much to keep an open heart. It put the fear in me that I wasn't worthy of being loved by anyone, so I decided to try to protect myself from facing the pain of my unlovability. I would stay quiet, not have any problems, and survive.

Along with the survival strategies came the pain of emotions. The pain of losing my status as a family member. The fear of my dad's next drinking binge. These things birthed cycles of pain in me that I couldn't resolve.

As I got older, I was a child of benign neglect. My brother was too, but he developed a different coping strategy. He acted out. Neither of us got any real attention from our parents. Little nurture and mostly no punishments either. We were good kids with good grades, so my parents didn't have the common complaints or problems with us. They had their own dysfunctions. My mom suffered from a nearly crippling obsessive-compulsive disorder, which often paralyzed her. Again, as it was my only experience of family, I just thought it was "normal."

My brother acted out by having lots of problems. I think since we were both attention-starved, he went for the "if I am not going to get positive attention, I will get negative attention" strategy. He got sick a lot and acted out emotionally—and he did get lots more attention. I, seeing how this further destabilized what I saw as an unstable family, decided to ask for nothing. Between my parents' dysfunction, my dad's work time, and my brother's issues, there was nothing left for me. I was just terrified that one day my dad would come home drunk and pack up his bags and leave for good. The times that I hid his keys and then followed him past the neighbors' houses at 2:00 in the morning, begging for him to come home, as he stormed angrily up the empty street with his suitcase toward who knows where, were things that I never wanted or expected to face.

As I grew up, the combination of meeting the conditions that people required of me in order to feel good, and avoiding feeling the sting of rejection when they told me that I was bad, became what I thought was how the world worked. Through repetition and habit, it would literally become the world pulled over my eyes that completely blinded me to the truth.

Remember, it is only after age 7 that we have the capacity to start exploring the world and comprehend what happens to us—but we rarely see what is happening within us. We don't realize that others' beliefs about us, what we believe about ourselves, and the emotions we feel deeply affect our minds and bodies.

I realize now that my conclusions about these events are just part of my perspective. They shaped my beliefs around alcohol, family dynamics, self-worth, and trust. That is the thing with perspective. It's unique to your life. It's your story. In that story, there are good times and bad.

The difference is that the good times don't hold us back. I remember great birthday parties and children's events that my parents created for my brother and me. There were amazing Christmases and memorable celebrations with both my mom and dad. We had wonderful times watching musicals like *My Fair Lady* and *The Sound of Music* with my mom, and watching baseball and playing catch with my dad. Most of the time we spent together was good.

But it's not the good times that we struggle with. It's the conclusions and emotions left from the hard times that stay with us. Every pain that we have not let go of limits our possibilities, distorts our perspective, and biases our choices and decisions. To get free from the limitations, we must learn how they work.

DISCOVERING THE TWO PATHS

It's not that we all don't share the same problems and the same answers; we are just never taught their functions. We are all taught a bunch of beliefs and definitions, but we never examine how they work. Just believe what your mom and dad and your teachers say, or those at church, and you get a reward. Disagree, disobey, or question, and you get punished. We are told how things are and how they should be. That is different from being taught and encouraged to follow our curiosity and empowering us to learn how things actually function. We can only begin to change when we learn how things function instead of just stopping at defining them.

There is a fun story about how this mistake is taught. There are plenty of different variations of this story, but the one I heard is called "The Legless Chicken."

A mother is cooking a chicken for dinner. Before cooking it, she removes the legs. Her daughter asks, "Why do you take the legs off before you cook it, Mom?" The mother replies, "That's the way my mom did it. Every time she ever cooked a chicken, she always took the legs off first." This didn't satisfy the daughter's curiosity, so she asked again, "But why?" Her mom couldn't answer the question, and so she called her own mom and asked why she always removed the legs of the chicken before she cooked it. Her mom just said that was the way that *her* mother had done it.

Finally, it is revealed that the reason the mom who started this family tradition several generations back removed the legs from the chicken was that the chicken was too big to fit in her pot.

In a nutshell, this is childhood. We are all taught things that we don't question and often repeat the mistakes that we are taught, much longer than we need to. We don't realize that we are creating our own realities. A lens through which we assess and gauge the world, as well as ourselves and others. An incomplete set of information, including all our rules, permissions, rights, wrongs, shoulds, and shouldn'ts. A full record of what we were rewarded for as well as what not to do to avoid punishments.

All of these things are unique to our experience and worldview. Our perspective is based on our experiences, our conclusions, and our beliefs about good and bad, right and wrong. The problem is, we just don't realize that our perspective is only about us. Each person's perspective is unique; no one's limited perspective encompasses the truth for anyone else. I am reminded of the summary of that quote from the movie The Matrix: "Do you want to know what the Matrix is? *The Matrix* is the world pulled over our eyes that blinds us to the truth."

THE TWO PATHS: PERCEPTION VERSUS REALITY

What are we taught from the moment we are born? We are taught what things mean. We are taught what things mean by those who are older and supposedly wiser than we are. Those in "authority." When we are born, the world is a complete unknown. Just possibilities. Undefined and wonderful. As soon as we are old enough, we are taught language. Words and their definitions. The birth of the intellect.

Once we have language, we begin creating meaning. Once we begin to internalize language, we develop an internal dialogue called thinking. We learn to construct and conceptualize. Remember that, as children, we are completely unable to care for ourselves and we don't know how to learn. We are literally curious and undefined sponges. Full of creativity and energy. Always curious about what that is or what this does. This is where we get into trouble, without having the ability to discern things yet. For our first seven years and beyond, our world is defined for us by other people who had concepts taught to them by others, who had their concepts taught to them, and so on and so on.

In essence, we are about to learn to cook the chicken without its legs. We are going to be taught definitions, stories, and beliefs about ourselves and the world by people who are passing on what they have been taught by someone else. Concepts and definitions without examination. Without ever asking the questions that can help us learn or examine how things work, we are left with assumptions. Form without function. The assumption of unexamined belief, passed down through the conditional love of others. The second half of the twofold problem: belief without functionality.

Worse yet, we are taught not to question. We are rewarded for agreeing or giving the right answers and punished for asking too many questions or giving the wrong answers. Meanwhile, we are being taught the limitations of the understanding of the people we meet, and taught to defer to them for the answers.

Very few people go deeper into how things work. They just pursue the rewards by giving the "right" answers and learn to avoid the punishments that result from the wrong answers. This really isn't learning. It's mimicry. Monkey see, monkey do.

As children, the conditioning of doing what others say and accepting what they tell us is true is our only option. We are taught to suppress our vibrant, curious enthusiasm by being punished for having it and rewarded for suppressing it. We are told that by replacing it with someone else's beliefs around good and bad, we will be more acceptable to our families and others.

After we wear this caricature for a while, the people who have labeled us and given us their requirements to follow stop seeing behind it. Thanks to neuroplasticity, it becomes part of habitual neurology. Other people don't see us anymore. Tragically, we also forget who we truly are. This process conveys to us that we are not wanted for ourselves—people only want us to pretend to be what they want. The real us isn't good enough to be loved. This is the first painful lesson of conditional love. Combine that with the unrealized process of conclusions drawn from it, and we create unrealized beliefs. A world pulled over our eyes that blinds us to the truth.

I was an energetic, kind, and gentle kid. I wanted to connect that loving kindness with my parents and other people. I loved just feeling alive, whether I was good at things or not. Like most kids, I loved making up stories and creating things out of Legos and Play Doh, and I was playful and curious. I was terrible at the visual arts, though.

My Play Doh creations were always lumpy and kind of leaned to one side. My Lego creations never came out as I had imagined them. In art class at school, my toothpick bird's nest came out much more like a toothpick bird coffin. I knew I wasn't good at it, but I still liked the feeling of total engagement. Where you just lose yourself in the process by focusing on what you are doing so completely that the world goes away.

One day an amazing thing happened in art class. We were given a project that really worked for me. By some strange miracle, my projects were coming out exactly as I imagined them. We were given thin copper squares and used tracing paper to trace something, an image that we would transfer to the thin copper sheet. I was never great at tracing but that day, it went well. We had to use a wooden tool to buff out the image after we transferred it to the copper sheet and I was amazed!

I had decided to make images for my parents: a horse for my dad and a dog for my mom. Not only did they come out looking like an actual horse and dog, they also had intricate details. Almost like shading was coming out as I worked the wooden tool into the copper sheet. It gave my project a three-dimensional look, and to this very moment I have no idea why it worked so well.

I was so excited to give them to my parents. We all have a sense of our abilities and I knew I was no Picasso, but this time I was. I was the proud Picasso of whatever this art thingy was. I had dismissed what the art teacher had said this magical art form was called, since I had already assumed my imminent failure. On this day, however, I had two works of proud perfection to share. I felt such a sense of accomplishment and excitement! I couldn't wait to share that with my parents.

I got home and was so careful on the bus to make sure that nothing put pressure on them to flatten out the images. My abnormally decent creations arrived intact, and I presented them with flourish and cere-mony. In my mind, this was a rare and special moment. My visual arts projects never worked...EVER. This was a triumph. I could finally give my parents something of value.

They both accepted them, but it was immediately clear that my proud and perfect projects didn't matter to them. They were distracted by whatever they were distracted with, and all three of us missed out on that genuine, open-hearted connection I was hoping for. I was crushed that they didn't, or couldn't, see what the pieces meant to me. It hurt way more when I found them squashed flat in the top of the garbage when they told me to take it out the next day.

In terms of the conditional love that I was raised with to that point, I was hopeful that since these offerings had turned out exactly as I had imagined, and I had thrown my entire focus and heartfelt effort into them, somehow that would be conveyed to my parents. After all, once I learned that their loving me or caring about me was based on some requirements that I did or didn't know, as well as their moods, there was always a performance standard that had to be met.

I had been so full of excitement, not only because something I usually sucked at had turned out well, but because I knew I couldn't have done better. It was my best offering, and it wasn't enough to get their attention, let alone their love. When I found my projects pressed flat by newspapers in the garbage, the message and conclusion that I drew was that doing my best or not, perfect project or not, they simply didn't, and wouldn't, care.

In the mind of a child, a parent who is distracted by their own personal worries and concerns doesn't compute. A child's perspective is far more limited than the capacity of an adult. It never occurs to a kid that mom and dad might be worried about the bills, or the never-ending to-do lists of managing a household, let alone their own relationship. I was only trying to get the loving attention that I rarely got.

Think about the effect a parent has on a child when using conditional love or not paying attention, lost in personal thoughts and beliefs. It impacts the way we think the world works by extension. When my parents were lost in their thoughts and didn't notice when I was trying to truly connect with them, I learned that loving me was secondary; there were more important things.

When my parents rewarded me for being a "good" boy or punished me for being "bad," the conditions that had to be met to be loved taught me that is how actual love worked. You withhold love to get what you want and deny it when you don't. Love was a tool to use to get what you want. That isn't even love. It's rejection and manipulation.

For me as a kid, it was conveyed to me that there was some inherent flaw. Something wrong inside of me that needed to be fixed. Neither my parents nor anyone else would love me until I was acting the way they thought I should. The fact that I was a kind-hearted, genuinely loving little kid didn't matter.

I remember watching the game show *The Price is Right*. I loved that show! Every time anyone won anything and got excited, I got excited for them! When someone got really excited, I would run through the whole house literally jumping with joy. I saw and felt how happy they were, and I wanted to make other people happy like that, so I would try to share that energy and excitement. Most of the time, my exuberance only seemed to annoy my parents and other grown-ups. That made my exuberance risky. To risk that kind of total exuberance could move from annoying them to being punished, so I learned that being too happy was "wrong."

Over time, my genuine self turned into who I was taught to be. All of that curiosity, energy, wonder, and excitement eventually got replaced by habitual suppression of my loving, curious, excited heart—transformed into beliefs about how I had to be in order to be accepted by others. I had learned that I had to earn love from others, and that the natural love I felt toward myself, my family, and the world was wrong.

From that moment on, love became work. I was taught to think that we all need to earn back what is lost. The constantly changing circumstances and differing judgments and labels from others replaced actual loving and caring, and that applied to everyone. That was how the world "worked."

To feel okay, we need the permission of everyone else, or they can take their love away as well. The connection that loving and trusting provides is replaced by a fear of the consequences of meeting—or not meeting—the ever-changing conditions and requirements put upon us by every person that we meet.

We must now try to be acceptable to our parents and friends, our teachers, and relationships. We are not enough. We have to become something different to each person. So, we learn to be dishonest. When we have to toe the line of the legless chicken and are not allowed to explore and follow things to their function, we are taught that truth doesn't matter. Just conforming to the desires of others is the way back to happiness.

That is what really happens to all of us. Have you heard of the 10,000-hour rule? It's the idea that to master anything, you need 10,000 hours of practice. That is 416.67 24-hour days. While we are growing up, we all get to master what others require us to learn. By age 7, we have all invested well over 10,000 hours that are unavoidable, as we are born into total disempowerment through circumstance. Our first and perhaps deepest misunderstanding is that we do not get to choose. We are put in situations in which we are forced to disown ourselves, to shape ourselves to fit the requirements of others. To conform. Our journey is not ours, it's dependent on satisfying others.

This is a cycle that we live out for the rest of our lives. In our work, our institutions of authority, our relationships, and the way we see ourselves.

Myriad interesting studies have been done to try to evaluate this shift in perspective. In education, for example, they often want to do studies to determine if they can identify the next up-and-coming batch of geniuses so they can fill the world's ever-growing need for innovation. New engineers, new ideas, and new scientists to create future technologies and advancements. In all the studies, they try to identify the characteristics that a child would need to be a future genius—but who are the ones defining "genius?"

So many forms of intelligence have been recognized that nearly every child begins with genius potential in some form. Can anyone truly determine the potential of any child, or any person, or can we only encourage or discourage their development? What are the actual effects of standardized testing and imposed, standardized curricula? Do they encourage or discourage the creativity and curiosity that come naturally to all of us as children?

We don't need to believe or disbelieve it. Just look at the problems in the schools: the steady decline in performance in math and the sciences. The dropout rates. Look at the shortfall of engineers, innovators, and scientists who are coming out of the education system at every level. Look at the impact of one-size-fits-all testing, of gifted children not being allowed to advance in accordance with their capabilities.

Being taught how to be, and taught that the only answer that matters is the desired answer, is just another form of being taught the legless chicken. This is the false premise that we all begin with. The combination of conditional love and unexamined beliefs. The demand is to make this process work, but this process is rooted in something subtler that can never work. It's underneath the stories and the emotions. It's in the replacing of reality with belief.

THE SECOND HALF OF THE MISTAKE:
MISTAKING PERSONAL PERCEPTION FOR REALITY

The emotions that I felt, and the stories I told myself about them, made up what I believed was reality. It's only by accepting the stories and their emotions and agreeing with them that we replace the possibilities of understanding with our perspectives. The key is that we have to agree with the stories and the painful emotions for them to hurt. We don't realize that we are not our stories or emotions. We have emotions; we create stories. The personal why and the personal because. Judgments and definitions.

When an event happens, we react to it, define it, and give it meaning. Events are just events. Feelings are just feelings. It is our thoughts and emotions and the stories that come with them that tell us otherwise.

No one can make you feel inferior
without your consent.
—Eleanor Roosevelt

I did an experiment with my buddy. I wanted to show him how flexible our stories and judgments are. I said to him, "My friend, you are a wonderfully curvaceous, interesting-smelling, exotic, obese woman." He laughed and, knowing me, was like... "That is exactly who I am." I followed it up with this: "And your father never loved you." He paused then, and I explained that we all have to agree for something to hurt.

What we believe, and the emotions that arise, are just information. To learn how things work, we must question and observe what is happening when emotions come up. Who we were taught to be isn't who we are. Our perspectives are not actual reality.

As children, we are like blank canvases. We can paint whatever we want onto the canvas, knowing that there are many possibilities for that canvas. We have that childhood love of play and exploration. Boundless curiosity. If we want a different picture, we can start over with a new canvas. But when we are defined by those around us, we no longer define ourselves moment to moment on new canvases. We begin to see ourselves as fixed, like a photograph—a frozen image of a rushing waterfall—where we once flowed freely. The waterfall is not dynamic, it's not moving. It's fixed. Permanent. Just the way things are. A belief about a waterfall.

Instead of painting our own pictures, pictures are painted of us by others. Remember when our moms made us wear some of those horrid childhood clothes? Once we put on those clothes, we are never allowed to take them off. We walk around wearing what someone else wanted and acting as they wanted, only to get affirmed or denied by each person that we come across. Each person believes they can paint a different version of us—depending on their personal likes and dislikes—on an increasingly cluttered canvas. With each new requirement and each new painter, we are moved further and further away from who we truly are.

This is the result of unexamined belief. While conceptualization and constructing thoughts are fine, they are limited. Thoughts can only think about more thoughts. Once we decide how something is, all other possibilities are immediately excluded. We believe this is how things are. Period.

No man ever steps in the same river twice.
—Heraclitus

There is no data or study that says reality is fixed; quite the opposite. Reality teaches everyone that moment to moment, there is only change. Every cell in our body, the oxygen we breathe, each beat of our heart, everything is in a constant state of change and variability. Nothing is ever as it was.

When our perspectives of the world and our perceptions of ourselves become fixed, there are no longer any possibilities. Whereas all beliefs are nouns, reality is a verb. Life is always lifeing.

It is hard for us to see this at first. We are all well past our 10,000 hours of training to be experts at defining ourselves and others through the eyes of conditional love. It's our most long-standing practice. Our deepest habits. Habits that are all unconscious to us.

All these things at one time had a learning curve. We have to consciously spend the time to figure them out. Once we do that, we get more skilled at using them more quickly and efficiently. We get better at what we practice, whether it be playing a musical instrument or lying. Eventually, if we practice long enough to form a habit, we are no longer aware that we are practicing.

We then play the instrument; we weave the web of deception. We perform. It is the same for all those hours of childhood. What did we have to do to be acceptable to our parents and other people? Who do we have to be now, day by day, to be acceptable to ourselves and those around us? Is it possible to satisfy every last requirement from work, from the never-ending to-do list at home, and from our relationships with friends and family? What if that is the legless chicken that we are all taught in childhood? Is it ever possible to take a false premise and make it true?

What if all the pain that we struggle with, and the reason nothing seems to work, is simply that no one can make the dysfunction of conditional love and personal beliefs into functional truth? What if, for all this time, we have unknowingly been trying to make virtual reality into actual reality? It would be decades before I saw that the difference between reality and the personal Matrix is the difference between belief and function.

Growing Up in the Matrix
Act Two:
Trying to make the roots
of dysfunction function

We do not see things as they are.
We see things as we are.
—*Rabbi Shemuel ben Nachmani*

I NEVER REALIZED THAT I WAS IMMERSED in the beliefs I had unknowingly created in those first seven years. Hell, I had no idea that beliefs existed at all, let alone that I had created them or accepted them from others. I had absolutely no idea that they were running my life.

Primarily what I believed from early childhood was that this is how the world works: To be accepted and to be okay, you must satisfy all the requirements and conditions put upon you by everyone else. Only then can anyone love or accept you, and only then should you dare to accept yourself.

I also thought this is how you show people that you love them: you give them the version of you that they want and never give them what they don't want. According to this false paradigm, conditional love is the key to loving others and yourself. It's also how you find freedom. Once you make everyone happy, once you solve all the problems that they have and you have and all the problems out in the world, then you can finally be happy. Not only would I learn later how wrong this was, but I would learn that this was expected of everyone.

Making a different version of myself for each person was like a game of make-believe. I had no idea that my childhood skill at playing make-believe was the way all beliefs are created.

Each time I got punished, any time I disappointed someone, the emotions felt terrible. When I was a kid I didn't know how to recognize negative emotions. It's not like while I was playing with my toys, I was contemplating psychology. I did the only thing that I was taught to do. I would meet all the requirements of everyone else to be a "good" boy, and then I would be okay.

I don't know about you, but in my childhood I had to learn to lie to try to protect myself and my good heart from being hurt or judged negatively by others. It's bigger than just me, though. Who do we become when we lie?

> *A lie is the truth said in fear.*
> —*Yogi Bhajan*

I am not asking for definitions or judgments. I am asking what is going on within our hearts and minds when we lie. What motivates us to lie? What is going on in our neurology? What if we aren't even conscious of what is going on while we are doing it because we had to learn to lie as children? How can we recognize what is going on if we have been practicing meeting the requirements of conditional love since before we had the mental capacity to realize it? What if I wasn't kidding when I said that we are all born into our own version of the Matrix?

My childhood was not only confusing, but also deeply painful. Every parent teaches their children to be like them to some degree, giving the sense that truth is subjective—our actions please or trigger our parents, teachers, and others in authority. The requirements change based on each person and circumstance, and we learn to adapt to these changing sets of rules to navigate the world.

How can we feel that we have any inherent value when each person has a different set of rules to satisfy before we get rewards and avoid punishments? My dramatic and traumatic diaper change at my grandmother's house confused me in ways that I simply couldn't comprehend for years. The implications of that incident still come up in different ways today.

In my mind, I had filled hundreds of diapers. It was an unquestioned part of my early life. It was a simple requirement of biology and, until then, I had always done it without punishment. When I got punished for it, and in a humiliating way, that broke my little brain and hurt my loving heart. Suddenly, although all my other diaper ventures had been fine, that time I was being forcibly held down and yelled at like the family dog. What had I done wrong this time when every other time was fine?

That safe, warm, easy, deep connection to ourselves and those around us that we start out with as children can be denied at the whim of anyone. Even by soiling your diaper in the wrong way, you learn that something is wrong with you. Paradise is lost, and now you must figure out, with each person and each situation, how to regain it.

No longer are we vibrantly connected to explore the world. We now need not only permission to explore it, but guidance as to how to do so. After years of being labeled, punished, and rewarded to look like the paintings that others have painted of us, both we and the world seem to have become known quantities. We know how to play the game: someone else makes the rules and we try to follow them, but at the expense of our true-hearted selves. Our stories and emotions blend into beliefs and—like the legless chicken—after all those years of practice without ever examining the roots of those beliefs, we are unaware of their impact and how they are still running in the background like programs on a computer.

It is only much later that we begin to reexamine our legless chicken theories, but until then, we have only beliefs and the emotions that fuel them.

What actually happens mentally and emotionally when being loved is replaced by the conditioning required to receive love? First, we feel the emotional pain from the rejection. We feel pain about what we lost as well as the desire to regain it. Our minds generate all sorts of fears that something is inherently wrong with us, so we can't trust ourselves—we must disown ourselves and defer to others.

When we suppress our true hearts, we learn to externalize everything. We no longer feel okay without the approval or confirmation of others and begin searching for answers outside of ourselves. We become afraid of losing others' approval, and we desire to regain it when it is lost. The other side of the fear coin is anger. We begin to resent those who have made us feel this way, and we seek to punish them as we have been punished. This is the birth of what is called the duality, or the split: the fearful, disempowering sense of loss from conditional love and the simultaneous desire to regain what was lost. The pain and pleasure principle. This is the key to realizing the Matrix, but we will get to that in a bit.

The emotional pain of my parents' rejection birthed a fear in me that kept me up at night. I never again trusted my mom or my brother as I had before that day, even on the rare occasions when they said they loved me.

Until recently, I had no idea how deeply I denied myself love because I was conditioned as a child that I didn't deserve it unless I said and did what other people required. Since then, I have learned a bit and re-examined a good few of my legless chickens, as well as the negative emotions that sustain them. It takes some time to realize the two paths, but already as children, we are unknowingly immersed in them.

In simple terms, the true-hearted path is the path of healthy, loving emotions, combined with the ability to choose, free from promised threat or reward. Free from labels, judgments, and requirements. Free to question, to explore, and to learn to trust ourselves and others in the world around us. A world of true-hearted possibilities.

The other path is one of the false self, which is created to satisfy the requirements of others. A fall into the duality, where the fear created by conditional love, and the desire to regain it by meeting the requirements of others, compel us to deny our true hearts. To deny our humanity and replace who we are with how we should be. I can promise you this: the degree to which we desire the acceptance and approval of others is the degree to which we have been taught to reject ourselves in the past.

A useful indicator of our disempowerment is that everything becomes external. Our feeling of being okay no longer comes from our true heart; it is always based on something outside of ourselves. The views of other people can trigger us, and circumstances now determine if we are okay, replacing our innate sense of well-being and confidence.

The legless chicken fable and the cycle of fear dramatically affected my life as a child. We can all think of examples of our beliefs not matching reality. I think the best example that is close to universal is Santa Claus. If you were taught, as I was, that this magical figure was real, and if—but only if—you were a good boy or girl, he would climb down your chimney and leave you toys, then you know what it is to replace reality with belief.

Not to belittle Santa. Or belief, for that matter. When we leave those beliefs unexamined by making assumptions or being fooled by negative emotions, we can only make mistakes. This is a real gift when you realize that every misunderstanding and mistake is an opportunity to learn—to align with what is true. It's another chance to understand that the journey is about contrast, and without both truth and lies, pain and healing, we could never journey at all. The pain in our trauma is an invitation to heal, learn, and grow.

I had a particularly memorable experience with Santa. You see, I was a true believer. I was going to be really up there on the "nice" list, which meant everyone below me was less nice. I was going to be so nice that I would get all the rewards and none of the punishments. No naughty list for this kid. Only the good stuff.

I kept believing in Santa well past the age when most kids, through common sense, realize that there may be some flaws in this story of a man in a red suit delivering toys to all the "good" children in the world in one night. Not me. I wasn't even going to risk questioning the concept. That is naughty-list talk right there. Christmas was a time of magic. People were nicer to each other, everything was decorated and festive, and the snow and winter cold gave it all a warm, magical glow.

On top of that, there was the anticipation of presents. Presents and good food. Lots and lots of good food—chocolates, chips, and special dinners. My parents seemed to argue less as well. They were more willing to suppress their arguing because they had Christmas as the justification. Everything and everyone was better at Christmas.

And there was Christmas break. School would be out for up to two weeks, depending on how the days fell on the calendar. I remember one year, on the last day of school before Christmas vacation, I was at my locker, dumping off my books and getting ready to head to the bus to go home, when my friend Nick stopped at his locker nearby.

He wished me a good holiday break while he, too, took care of his locker needs. I didn't even hesitate. It was well known by everyone that Santa was real, so I asked, "What did you ask Santa for this year?" Nick paused. He looked over at me incredulously, as if he were assessing something, and then he asked me the impossible question. With a quick glance around to see who might be listening, he leaned toward me and whispered, "You know that Santa isn't real, right?" A million thoughts raced through my mind at once. I couldn't believe anyone could think that. How was I to believe something this ridiculous? Everyone knew that Santa was real!

The only response that I could muster was one born of years and years of unquestioned belief and emotional investment. I told Nick that not only was Santa real, but he'd better shut up. He, to his eternal credit, tried again. "Santa isn't real!" he whispered in pleading tones. I simply couldn't accept this blasphemy, and after I hissed another angry warning to shut up, I threw my very first punch.

I was around 13 or 14, and I didn't know how to throw a punch. Nick gave me one last exasperated plea, "Santa isn't real!" And then I stormed away.

Sadly, after that I was no longer friends with Nick. (Sorry, Nick.) It was, however, my first real understanding of the legless chicken story in my own experience. I had been taught about how things are, as well as how they should be, and never examined them. I had literally no idea that what I believed wasn't necessarily true. The story and the emotion I had invested in it had blinded me to the fact that I had adopted a false reality. My belief was not the truth.

> *It ain't what you don't know that gets you into trouble.*
> *It's what you know for sure that just ain't so.*
> *—Mark Twain*

I had created a reality that was useful to and about me alone. I'd formed a personal set of judgments, conclusions, decisions, and preferences that I wanted to be true and assumed everyone else agreed with them. That was how I knew that all was right with the world. If things that I believed in, like Santa, were true, and whatever else I believed in was affirmed, no matter the actual truth, I was okay with that, too.

I never questioned or understood the difference between who I was taught to be and how I was taught the world is, and how things actually were. That got in my way while I was growing up.

Without examining our beliefs and the emotions fueling them, we stand on a shifting patchwork of mixed reality. Not everything we were taught is false information, but not all of it is true, either. Santa taught me that. While I was growing up, things seemed really hit or miss until I began to see that I had to question everything for myself. No one ever taught me to look behind beliefs and emotions to see what is true.

> *We live in our minds and not in the world.*
> *—Suzuki Roshi*

I was walking around with a gigantic legless chicken named Santa. No one had ever challenged something I cared so much about. The magic and wonder, as well as the stories around Santa and Christmas, gave me the why and the emotions gave me the because. Of course Santa is real! The feeling that I had on Christmas morning said so. Listening to a beautiful version of "Silent Night" while I watched the snow drifting down to the ground by moonlight said so. I was never going to examine that concept because if I dared to question it, things might change. I could be punished. That naughty list was super real to me. To question Santa's existence meant facing the possibility of losing everything I loved about Christmas. An unrealized fear of loss and desire for gain. The pain and pleasure principle.

Everything that we need to realize is always right in front of us, but we can blind ourselves to it with our own personal Matrix of beliefs. When Nick challenged my precious legless chicken, he threatened that magical sense of wonder that I associated with Christmas. I didn't realize that my externalization tricked me into thinking that Nick was to blame, while it was really my own emotions that adorned that legless chicken. It was my own inner reaction that did all of that.

Over the years, my reaction to perceived threats began changing everything, once I began to question my assumed reality. It was my first clue that there was another reality that I didn't create—a reality that was unaffected no matter how much I wanted there to be a Santa. A reality that didn't care how much I believed or didn't believe. There was something behind beliefs called truth. A reality behind the Matrix.

THE GREAT DECEIVER

We are all taught in high school biology class that the threat response, also called the fight-or-flight response, is part of the primitive brain that is there to help us survive. It immediately activates when we are threatened, assessing whether the threat can be successfully fought off or if it would be better to run away as far and as fast as we can until we are safe.

This response is a cascade of biochemistry that affects our thoughts and emotions and our physical body and brain. Every aspect of us—mental, physical, and emotional—is altered when the fight-or-flight response is triggered. The transformation is completed in a microsecond.

It's not just a feeling. It's a complete, immersive shift of perspective, like looking through a pair of glasses that warp and change what we see. From thoughts and emotions to biochemical and physiological effects, everything we see and feel through this lens is completely and instantaneously distorted, but it all seems so real that we can mistake it for reality. This is an entry point to the Matrix. That false sense of reality pulled over our eyes that blinds us to the truth.

It's not that the fight-or-flight response itself isn't useful. If there is a bear—or someone with a gun—coming at you, this response can generate the adrenaline rush that you need to survive. The issue is that we get triggered when our personal beliefs are challenged or we challenge the beliefs of others. As it turns out, everyone has some version of how I felt about Santa, and they, too, are willing to fight or flee when it is triggered.

But the distortion of the negative emotions feels so real! The feeling immediately justifies the thoughts in the reaction. When my fight-or-flight brain got triggered, Nick wasn't challenging my unexamined beliefs, he was challenging truth itself! He was challenging America and Santa Claus. What would he challenge next, the existence of God?

Look at that logic. It's absolutely absurd, but when we react negatively to our limited perspectives being challenged, our clarity and objectivity give way to a perspective generated by a completely unknown part of us that is built into our biology, the part that tries to protect the limited self from harm. The part of our biology that generates all of our negative emotions. The threat response.

When the threat response is triggered, all the blood that is usually feeding the area of the brain where good decisions are made is redirected to our muscles so we can fight or flee for our lives. Functional intelligence has been measured during fight or flight, and we actually get incredibly dumber.

The average American's IQ is 98. When someone is threatened, their IQ can drop up to 30 points! Decision-making and the way we interpret the events and environment around us, as well as what we think about ourselves, is drastically altered.

Now, you can go and look that up and try to find that one person in that one study who reached that 30-point decline, or you can just look at your own experience. Remember a time when you got so mad that you said a hurtful thing you wish you hadn't said? Think of a time when fear did the opposite, and you held your tongue and stayed silent and afterwards wished that you had said something. Either way, were any of those words said out of kindness or compassion?

The IQ at which people are considered intellectually disabled is between 70 and 75. Reading comprehension can drop up to six grade levels, so interpreting things that you read or that people are saying—or your own thoughts, which are just words—is incredibly impacted as well. The degree to which we feel afraid or angry corresponds to the level of bad decisions we are willing to make. Have you ever heard of crimes of passion? This may be the reason for them.

It's not hard to find countless examples of people's negative reactions. Turn on any show about news or politics. Watch your favorite team play against their rival. What happens when the politics don't match ours or our team is losing or gets what we consider a "bad" call? What does it feel like if you agree or disagree with the politics or the calls from the referee? It's a function of the threat response. It's the pain-pleasure principle. We feel what we think are positive emotions when we get what we want, and the pain of negative emotions when we don't. It feels "good" to get your way, and "bad" not to.

If we slow down, we can see that the reactions in all those instances are made up of the same two elements: emotions that arise as we react and stories that seek to justify them. The feelings then justify the stories, as well as the thoughts and words used to justify the feelings in the reactions.

You do realize that all thoughts are just made up of words and that every word is made up by someone, right? We all had to learn to speak as children. We didn't come into this world pre-loaded with language and definitions. We were taught what and whom to believe. I also didn't realize that stories can stir emotions.

I didn't realize this when I was fighting for my belief in Santa. I never even thought about it. I just reacted when what I thought was true was challenged. It seems so unfair that we are born into a world we can't understand, a world that is totally defined by others who teach us their misunderstandings, which were taught to them by others with their misunderstandings, and then we get to deal with emotions that literally blind us to the truth. It's a complicated scenario—and then throw school and all the other responsibilities put onto us on top of that mess.

So now, we meet hundreds and thousands of other people who haven't examined their perspectives either, interacting and trying to learn how to avoid being punished or ridiculed or judged while getting the approval of others.

Thus, the world is full of unexamined legless chickens with limited individual perspectives, assumed to be the universal truth by those who believe them, and all are invested in their own emotions. If we, too, simply affirm their legless chickens, they will affirm ours. As long as we agree, they will treat us well, and if we disagree, they will find a way to punish or avoid us. Just like our parents and teachers. All of it justified by negative emotions, disguised by the cycle of the pain-pleasure principle. The desire for gain and the fear of loss.

So much of what we suffer in our lives comes from this misunderstood expression of the fight-or-flight response and the assumptions that come with it. My negative emotional reaction to Nick, as well as the emotionality that would bubble up when my other legless chickens and Santas were exposed or challenged. Each time reality didn't match what I believed, I had a negative emotional reaction, a sense of being threatened. All of it came from my limited personal story—the narrative of who I was and what I believed, which I thought had to be affirmed so I could feel good and never challenged. So I wouldn't feel bad.

It is the same with all our Santas and legless chickens. All our mental suffering, confused and fueled by the fear of loss and the desire to gain, unknowingly created by negative emotions generated by that same fight-or-flight response. Those powerful emotions and their impacts on our perspectives literally affect how and what we think, feel, and conclude. Without beginning to question negativity as a first step, we can completely mistake our beliefs for reality.

I remember so many things from my school days, mostly the things that made me uncomfortable. I don't remember many great moments. Due to my unstable home, I became a worrier. I was super stressed. In school, as at home, I learned the rules and requirements, met them, and just tried to stay out of the way. That didn't mean that life wouldn't intervene and force me to experience what I wished to avoid.

I once had an assignment that I can only assume was to help kids make friends with each other. We had to look around the classroom and pick someone we would like to be friends with. After drawing a picture of that person, we were to present it to them and ask to become their friend.

Easy, right? Well, I mentioned to you earlier that I was terrible at the visual arts. Drawing was no exception. I chose a kid who looked friendly. I even thought his skin tone was cool. I was pale with a bit of a ruddy complexion; his complexion had an orange tint. Almost a tan with a hint of orange. For my drawing, I aimed for realism.

I went for the orange crayon. It was the closest that I could think of, and I wasn't any expert at blending colors, so, with my tongue sticking out in concentration, I began my masterpiece. Who knows, we might become best friends! I was doing my best. Doing your best doesn't mean that the results will be good.

My total lack of talent in drawing and my poor overall skills in visual arts conspired to make my masterpiece look more and more like…a pumpkin.

On top of that, I was running out of time. The teacher had just signaled that we had five more minutes left before we would meet our new friends, and I was frantic. I grabbed an eraser and tried to reduce the pumpkin to more of a human face, but in my effort, I began to see other flaws. The head shape was all wrong. It was too round. The eyes certainly had no symmetry, and oh…the spacing of them!

Even with my total concentration and desire to do my best, I had ended up with this. The teacher asked us to stop and get ready to meet our new friends. Hoping that my picture wasn't too bad, I went up and introduced myself to Bob.

I was nervous and hoping for the best as I handed Bob my rather cubist interpretation of his visage. To my surprise, not only did Bob not like it, he was incredibly insulted and wanted to fight me after school.

The teacher could see that we weren't quite bonding, and with tears of upset in his eyes, Bob showed her the mockery that I had presented to him as an offer of friendship. In his mind, it was an insult for someone to view him like that. It was no different than my reaction to Nick and Santa. The only difference was that in this scenario, I was Nick.

I pled my case to the teacher and apologized profusely to Bob. The teacher could see that I wasn't being a jerk, I was just terrible at art. Bob and I never did become friends in any meaningful or lasting way.

His emotional reaction to my artwork was not what I had intended at all. When things like this happen to us—when we feel that negative reactivity come up in us—it feels real, and we think it's what the other person meant for us to feel. We don't realize that they are just reacting from their personal perspective, right?

From Bob's perspective, I was making fun of how he looked. From my perspective, I was doing my best to make a new friend. To me, Nick was talking craziness and threatening to violate one of my favorite things on the planet. To Nick, I was about to embarrass myself to anyone else that I told, and he was just trying to be a real friend and protect me. My reaction when Nick told me the truth that challenged my belief felt terrible. The negative emotions from the threat response are only pain. I couldn't face it and so I lashed out at him.

We just don't realize where personal perspective ends and reality begins. How can we, given our distorted introductions to the world? It's as if that painting of ourselves done by others, imposed upon us as children, becomes like a shadow self. It becomes the thing that we are taught to follow without realizing that to be led by a shadow, we have to face directly away from the light.

What we don't realize that what is going on inside of us is neuroplasticity. Our brains and nerves are constantly forming habit patterns, actual circuits that create feedback loops based on what thoughts we think and what emotions we feel. How much more challenging is it to distinguish personal belief from reality when we have developed loops that offer instant responses to stimuli? We react before we can begin to process what is happening in real time. An automatic, habitual response so fast that we are unaware of what is happening. Our neurology is built over time, and we are not conscious of our participation in its creation. The birth and development of a false sense of self continues until we begin to look at it in a different way. Our own personal Matrix. A series of habits and patterns, still trying to tell us how things are and how they have to be—within and outside of ourselves—so we can be mentally and emotionally okay. It's in all our stories and all our emotions, once we look at their function.

> *To define is to limit.*
> —*Oscar Wilde*

We are all taught that to learn is to memorize. To define and label. To judge right from wrong based on our personal definitions and memorizations and the definitions and conclusions of others.

If you and I have any chance to grow, we need to move from the process that we were all taught—memorization, definition, and conclusions about who we, and those around us, should be and how the world should be—to a perspective based solely on how things function. The path of wisdom. Maybe that is a loaded word. By wisdom, I only mean function. How it works in relationship. The application of a concept. While a concept is a noun, living it is a verb. We all think we know the definition of dancing as a concept, but the only way to experience the truth of how closely we can embody and live that concept is by dancing. There is a big difference between reading a book about building a house and actually building one.

* * *

There is another path: the one with all the wisdom. The big T truths that function the same for everyone. No one owns it or can change it, regardless of their belief. It is not the false knowing of the legless chicken.

He who knows does not speak;
He who speaks does not know.
—Lao Tzu

LABELS VS. FUNCTION: THE PARABLE OF THE WISE MAN

My uncle once told me a story about a wise man who had a fine stallion. Everybody said how lucky he was to have such a horse. "Maybe," he said.

One day the stallion ran off. The people said the wise man was unlucky. "Maybe," he said.

The next day the stallion returned, leading a string of fine ponies. The people said it was very lucky. "Maybe," the wise man said.

Later, the wise man's son was thrown from one of the ponies and broke his leg. The people said it was unlucky. "Maybe," the wise man said.

The next week, the chief led a war party against another tribe. Many young men were killed. But because of his broken leg the wise man's son was left behind, so he was spared.

What effect does our judgment or opinion have on reality? If the wise man chose, like the people, to judge or label each situation as good or bad, does that make it true? This story offers a direct comparison of the two paths: the path of the limited personal perspective versus the truth of the whole. One path creates beliefs according to its limited perspective and projects them onto the world, and the other path knows that judgments and labels have no impact on reality. Did my hardcore belief in Santa make Santa real? Did my conclusion about being removed from the family and becoming the family pet make that true, or was it my conclusion based on negative emotions that made it seem and feel real to me? Did people suspecting that my dad may have been into penguin porn, instead of just being exhausted, make that true? Oh wait, that story is almost here. We haven't gotten there quite yet.

Given all our personal beliefs, judgments, and emotions, all we can do is reinforce our limited personal perspectives and biases, further distancing ourselves from a reality that our beliefs have no effect on, but that we can only align or be out of alignment with. Do our conclusions and judgments ever have any impact on reality?

The people in the parable who labeled everything as lucky or unlucky were at the mercy of their personal perspectives and their definitions of which outcomes were "good" or "unlucky." Like them, if we constantly judge everything based on our limited perspectives and expect our judgments to have any impact on reality, we will constantly be upset—as I was with Nick, and Bob was with me.

How do our experiences and conclusions change if we become balanced like the wise man, rather than constantly defining or being defined by situations or other people as good or bad? Give it a try and notice what happens when you just let reality stand without judging or defining it.

THE HIGHER PATH OF WISDOM

Concept is fine, but wisdom is concept in motion. Pure function. We were all taught at school that memorizing primarily constitutes learning. We were rewarded with good evaluations for giving the answers required of us. We are taught that this is the truth of the world, but if we have a functional understanding of the two paths, we can begin to see the difference between limited self-made perceptions and actual reality.

The two paths are totally invisible until we start questioning our assumptions. Moving from defining, labeling, and judging to living the concepts with a sense of curiosity and possibility. It is hard to see at first, because of the process and time and emotions we have invested in our beliefs. How much neurology have we invested in these feedback loops? All these patterns have become habits that we aren't conscious of anymore. We must stop making things in our image and examine their function.

THE PARABLE OF THE TWO PATHS

We are made up of two distinct natures, mirrored back to us by our two distinct neurological pathways. Fight or flight and rest, digest, and recover. One path that splits into the duality of the threat of loss and the desire to gain, avoiding pain and experiencing pleasure, and one that heals and unifies. It is in their function that outcomes are determined. We all have these two paths within us.

The two paths are in everything we do. They're in our books, movies, histories, and music. We have no idea which path we are on until we learn to recognize how each one functions.

The difference between intellect and wisdom extends out a good bit further than that, as things flow from thought to word to action. The intellect never gets to put the concept into action. It draws a conclusion from its limited personal perspective, and that can easily become a legless chicken.

The path of wisdom is the path of living concepts by putting them into motion. Embodying them. Showing how well you can build a house, instead of thinking and debating the concepts. Knowing, like the wise man, that conclusions about concepts are arbitrary. The only thing that matters is how well you can build the house.

The wisdom path is the path of not knowing. No hard conclusions and a certainty that there is always more to learn. Curiosity and inquiry. You realize that you have your personal, limited perspective like everyone else. Your beliefs are not absolute truths that apply to everyone in the world; they are useful map markers that help to guide you on your personal journey. Your current level of understanding. A personal point of view for your unique journey alone toward truth.

There is an insightful wisdom story from the Native American tradition called "The Two Wolves." It addresses the second half of the twofold confusion. Whereas the legless chickens are the unexamined thoughts that have become assumptions, the wolves are what happens when we fuse those legless chickens with emotions. The fusion of heart and mind that creates belief.

THE PARABLE OF THE TWO WOLVES

An elder was telling the children a story about life. "A fight is going on inside of me," he said. "It is a terrible fight, and it is between two wolves.

"One wolf is full of anger, sorrow, envy, regret, greed, arrogance, self-pity, guilt, resentment, inferiority, lies, superiority, false pride, self-doubt, and ego. The other wolf is good. He is joy, peace, love, hope, serenity, humility, kindness, generosity, truth, compassion, and faith.

"This fight is going on inside of you and every other person, too."

The children thought about it and then one asked this question: "Which wolf will win?"

The elder paused thoughtfully and replied, "The one you feed."

All the wisdom stories point toward these two paths, and all of them are giving clues to the way things function. So much of the opportunity for true learning is lost when we are taught that learning comes through memorizing, drawing conclusions, and then defending that point of view to prove it is the right one.

A well-known and commonly misunderstood example is the wisdom teaching "judge not, lest you be judged." What if that is a statement of how things function? Have you ever been judged by someone and not felt like you wanted to judge them to balance the scale? Can you ever judge others without putting yourself above them? Which path do you think this comes from and which wolf does it feed?

When something is reduced to the intellectual process of simply defining what it means and not understanding its function, many of us just stop questioning; we look to reinforce our personal definitions by rewarding others for agreeing and punishing them when they disagree.

Endless cycles of threats and rewards, regardless of function, unknowingly feed the wrong wolf. In fact, all the true wisdom teachings show us the same dynamics in hopes that we can see how the world works.

So much of what we call religion or spirituality is just finding wisdom behind interpretations. Not stopping at repeating the concept, but finding the way to move that concept into function, setting that fixed definition back into motion.

It's no different with the emotions. We have the basic three on either side. On the true path we have Love, Peace and Joy. On the false path we have Anger or Fight, Fear, and Flight and Sadness, which is also called Freeze. Fight, flight, and freeze. Anger, Fear, and Sadness, combined with the false "positive" emotions that come up when we get what we want and avoid loss. The relief of avoiding punishment and the temporary good feeling of getting the reward. The duality of the fear of loss and the desire for gain that arises when the fight-or-flight response gets triggered.

That response gets triggered every time our personal, limited perspectives feel threatened, or gets affirmed whether they be real or imaginary.

The confusing part is that each time we get what we want, our brain gets a dopamine hit. Dopamine is the "feel good" chemical, and it is released each time we are affirmed or get what we want. That, in time, creates neurology, which patterns into our physiology. On the flip side, each time we don't get what we want, or are not affirmed in what we believe to be "true," the threat response can be triggered, releasing its own cascade of cortisol, norepinephrine, and adrenaline—the stress hormones.

There are hundreds of examples in each of our lives. When Nick contradicted my personal beliefs and stories about Santa, all that I loved about Christmas felt threatened. Focus on that word, FELT. Each time my dad came home late and had been drinking, and when my mom did the diaper thing. All those events and hundreds more triggered my fight-or-flight response, that dualistic cycle of trying to avoid the pain of each loss and the desire to feel good again. Those negative emotions then generated negative thoughts.

If Santa wasn't real, what about God? What else did my parents lie about? What else did I believe in that might not be true? My dad's drinking felt so destabilizing and unpredictable—what would happen if the family fell apart? If my mom was willing to do that to me with a diaper, how could I trust her enough to be close to her again?

Fear and worry became my baseline thoughts and emotions, and I wanted to find a way to end that pain. I remember when we first started giving speeches in school. I was in fifth grade and, like I said, I was a worrier. I was so nervous about so many things. We were asked to do class presentations. Just a few weeks before a nurse had come in, dressed in her nurse's outfit, and given a talk about how stress could be assessed simply by touching a sheet of what looked like plastic and holding it for 30 seconds. The biochemical reactions from stress could be measured through the skin with this particular kind of plastic and would be shown on a shading scale as it moved from light to dark, and a measurement scale moving from bottom to top.

The nurse told us that, according to doctors, stress was a factor in over 90 percent of all diseases. That didn't help me at all. Now I worried that I was going to get some strange disease because I was so stressed. I could feel my palms getting clammy as I saw her produce the plastic measuring tool.

She handed out the strange sheet of plastic and let it circulate through the class while she continued talking, but I don't remember any of what she said past that, because I was freaking out about what that scale would say about me. I was also worried that the other students might see me worrying. Anyone who has been through school knows what can happen if other kids detect a weakness.

I saw that plastic thing approaching at the head of my row. My heart was pounding and I was starting to sweat. Finally it was my turn, and as soon as I touched the plastic the gauge not only climbed right up the scale—it turned black.

It was no shocker. I knew I was stressed, but seeing that external measure made me feel worse. It was as if something outside of me measuring my stress meant that I couldn't deny or control it on the inside anymore. Others would see what was happening, and then everyone would find out. Talk about even more to worry about. Ironically, I got so stressed out about that stress test that I nearly passed out.

I didn't know what to do with all the stress and anxiety that I had around school. I just knew that it felt awful. Even besides the standard cruelty and the school friendships, it was an experience that ranged from uneventful to horrific. Just like the emotions we all have most of the time.

I had no way to look at fear objectively. When we get the facts without wisdom, they ring hollow anyway. I was taught that we had two nervous pathways—the sympathetic and parasympathetic pathways—which are activated when we are stressed or relaxed. Knowing a concept doesn't change the way you react when your emotions get triggered, though.

You know from your experiences that what we call logic or rationality simply goes right out the window when we are triggered by our emotions. Later in life, I noticed that the same thing happened every time I struggled in a relationship or a job or even did poorly on a test, let alone getting lectured by a parent. You know what that feels like. It's all pain.

All our negative emotions hurt, and that pain is very similar to the pain of a physical injury. It hurts and we want the pain to end. It's truly amazing what goes on physiologically and mentally when we experience emotional pain. A cascade of chemicals, including cortisol, floods the tissues. If stress continues for an extended period, cortisol begins to break the tissues down. The body begins to destroy itself. Did you know that being chronically stressed for an extended period of time suppresses the immune system?

The mind attacks itself as well. The thoughts that we think become distorted, as if by a fun-house mirror. All around us, we see only threats and concerns. Things to worry about. Peace of mind is gone, and the ceaseless thinking about what to do and what will happen is all-consuming. The mind becomes blind to anything but ending the pain. Attack or defend, fight or flee. It's the stories that we merge with these emotions that limit our possibilities and cause us confusion and pain. The story is the why and the emotion becomes the because. The stories we tell ourselves, and the emotions we merge them with, get hardwired into our neurology over time, limiting or benefitting us depending on which emotional wolf we feed.

This didn't start as a full-blown problem. My fear of giving speeches in school didn't get better, as I had to speak more and more in different classes. Each time I had to speak, I got more and more nervous. Each time, I was unknowingly altering my neurology. Each time my fight-or-flight response to public speaking was triggered, I was unwittingly feeding the wrong wolf. How do you think those speeches went, knowing that our brain function and IQ drops 30 points when we are stressed?

After a while, the fear that arose merged with the idea of speaking publicly, and I developed a fear of public speaking. It's not like babies are born with road rage. All our limitations are first taught to us when we are young through the initial rejection of us by conditional love, which creates the root sense of fearful separation, and then we learn the process well enough to teach ourselves. It's not productive learning, though.

MISTAKING PERSONAL PERSPECTIVE FOR REALITY

You have probably heard the story of the blind men and the elephant. It is a story about a group of blind men, none of whom have never come across an elephant before. They must learn and conceptualize what an elephant is by touching it. Each man feels a different part of the elephant's body, but only one part, such as the trunk, the tail, or the tusk. Each one then describes the elephant based on his own limited experience, so their descriptions of the elephant are quite different from each other. In some versions each man suspects that the others are lying, and they come to blows. The moral of the parable is that humans claim absolute truth based on their limited, subjective experiences and ignore other people's limited, subjective experiences, which may be equally true.

PUTTING THE ASS IN ASSOCIATION

The process of self-limitation is always the same. We feel a negative emotion come up in a certain circumstance, as I did with public speaking, associate that feeling over and over again with a reason or story, the neurological connection develops, and the time between the stimulus and the negative emotional response gets shorter and shorter until all of a sudden, they merge into a reaction. We have the two components of every limiting belief: we have a reason (public speaking), and we have a verification of reality. This is how every person on this planet is tricked into believing that our limited, fearful perspective is actual truth.

I judged public speaking as awful, since that is how my nervousness felt when the fear came up; I focused on the anxiety, which inadvertently fed the wrong wolf, which then generated thoughts that told me I was risking my insecurities being discovered and I would be negatively judged, which generated more fear.

The feeling and the story made me forget that the feelings were generating the reasons. Again, it was conditional love. I had to meet the requirements of my classmates and the teacher to feel good and avoid their judgments, to not feel bad. The fear of loss and desire for gain.

I had no other choice. I had only been taught to externalize all of it because I was disempowered as a child. I had no clue that there was an alternate path, or that the path of negative emotions always and only came from my own perspective. That limited, personal perspective, however, as well as the parable about the blind men and the elephant, were about to give me one of my favorite memories about my poor, misunderstood dad—and penguins.

I had the most wonderful and complete experiences of the elephant and the legless chicken, as well as the two wolves—stories all wrapped up in one night while I was in high school, when my family decided to go and see a movie about sharks at the Omnimax Theater in Pittsburgh, Pennsylvania.

My mom was on board, so my dad decided that he would go along with the plan. Omnimax is a special type of filmmaking whereby they fill your total field of vision with the movie. The screen is contoured to include your entire field of vision. At the time, I had not realized that my vision had deteriorated to such an extent that I wasn't seeing most of it anyway, but it was something new to try and I thought sharks were cool.

We watched the shark documentary, and it wasn't as cool as I thought it would be. Both my mom and I were bored. I was going to lobby my mom to head out, but then an unexpected bonus feature on penguins came on afterward. I had no interest in penguins back then (unless they were talking about the hockey team), but we couldn't ask my dad to leave because there was no pause between movies. It just went straight into the penguins with no intermission.

For some reason, my dad had decided to sit by himself about a dozen rows behind everyone else, in the corner seat where the row ended at the wall. We were all bored, but it became fun to glance back and see him trying to stay awake. It was more fun to watch his head slowly droop as his eyes closed, then suddenly jerk up when he popped back to wakefulness, than it was to watch the movie. My mom started to watch him too, and it became our new form of entertainment. Watch a bit of the playful penguins, and then check on Dad.

The theater was a bit under half full, probably around 150 people in total. The shark movie itself might have been a bit of a bust, but the show that we were about to see was the real bonus feature.

Finally, the movie was over and the credits started to roll. I stood up and stretched, and my mom, who was right next to me, called back across the dozen or so empty rows to my dad.

"Jim! Were you jerking off during that movie?" Now, I knew what she was asking. We had seen my dad repeat that pattern of drooping and jerking himself upright at least a dozen times, but she didn't ask him if he was drifting off to sleep or if he was jerking himself awake. She had combined the two into a beautiful tragicomedy.

There was a pause among those in the drowsy crowd who overheard this. They seemed to perk up a bit, and I watched as they looked from her to him and back again with confusion and amusement etched all over their faces.

To make things worse, my mom was unaware that the words she was innocently directing at my dad were also a slang reference to masturbation. Beyond that, his decision to sit all the way in the back, completely alone, must have seemed a bit strange to the rest of the audience.

Mom repeated, "Jim! Were you jerking off during the movie?" I couldn't help but buckle over in laughter. The look on his face was a mixture of frantic pleading and horror. He began to wave his hands, shouting back, "NO, Stella! NO!" This only made my mom angry. From her perspective, she was just asking a simple question. She wasn't doing anything to make him react that way. She and I had both seen his efforts to stay awake during the penguin movie.

So she began to get more and more angry, loudly saying, "I saw you jerking off during that movie!" This was too much for me. I literally couldn't breathe. It was sublime. The misunderstandings. The miscommunications, the reactions of both my parents that only made things worse, and the small crowd of people slowly dispersing, some with scowls of judgment, others smirking, and a few looking angry.

I can only imagine what they were thinking as they left the theater. What was that chubby man doing all the way in the back while watching those playful penguins? Whatever they were thinking, I promise you that the least likely conclusion they drew was the truth: that my dad was just trying to stay awake and didn't want my mom getting mad at him for drifting off if he sat next to her.

I had gotten to glimpse the entire elephant. I saw all the individual, limited perspectives and how all of them, like the blind men, assumed they knew the whole truth of the situation. I knew why my mom was getting mad. I knew why my dad was horrified at what my mom was shouting at him. I knew from the looks on people's faces that they were reacting emotionally based on what they instantly judged was the reality of the situation. Seeing the whole elephant in that experience was beautiful!

When any event is happening, we all think that we are just assessing the situation. We can't see the filters or the assumptions. We aren't conscious of our biases, and we are easily washed away by our emotions. The story of the elephant is true. We are all blind, replacing reality with our limited information and conclusions.

I promise you that this is the only problem anyone ever has. We mistake our personal, limited perspectives for the truth. We create legless chickens with our intellectual assumptions and make them seem true with the duality of the negative path that splits into threats of loss and desires for gain, from the wrong-hearted wolf. You most likely can't see it yet. After all, we have all been trying to replace reality with our personal beliefs for as long as we have been alive.

It would literally be around 20 more years before I saw both parts of the lie that I was trying so hard to live. Both halves are in that parable about the three blind men and the elephant. I was totally immersed in my limited perspective and thought it was the whole truth. The other part was even more subtle. I didn't realize that the blind men's disagreement in that parable was the other side of the dysfunction that I couldn't make function.

The negative emotions that came up every time I reacted told me that those reactions were justified—that all my judgments and conclusions about other people and the world were right, just, and good, while anything that ever challenged or contradicted my limited perspective was wrong. Emotions just feel so real.

I thought that if I focused on both the thing that justified the emotions and the upset that I felt, they would resolve. That when I focused on the thoughts they were generating and the solutions they offered, I wasn't feeding the wrong wolf. I had been taught that focusing on the problem was how you find the solution.

It was only after I became aware of my reactions and stories that I began to unravel the puzzle of who I thought I was and who I had been taught to be. The answers are not in the stories and emotions; they are in how they function. Who are we when we are angry or afraid? We are lost to reality, washed away by a nature that we are only now beginning to see. The virtual reality of our personal beliefs pulled over our eyes that blind us to the truth.

The Function of Dysfunction: Unknowingly Feeding the Wrong Wolf

For the good that I would I do not:
but the evil which I would not, that I do.
—Romans 7:19 Paul of Tarsus

TRUMPETS PLEASE! OH, THERE IT IS! The universal problem that every person on the face of this planet suffers from, the one thing that creates all their conflict and pain. We mistake our limited, selfish perspectives for the whole truth, and when it is questioned or challenged we get upset. The way we believed the world should or shouldn't be feels threatened. The threat reaction floods us with negative thoughts and emotions from the legless chicken and the wrong-hearted wolf.

In a nanosecond, all our true humanity is replaced with a selfish caricature inhumanity that is as much as 30 IQ points dumber, and we are totally unaware of the switch. All our patience and kindness disappears.

Then the most insane thing happens. Instead of questioning our reaction, we redefine things based on that limited personal perspective, demanding that what we wish to believe be the truth.

As I did with Nick and Bob did with me, as well as the way my parents interacted at the theater and the other people in the audience no doubt thought they knew what was going on, we don't understand that we are lost in our limited perspectives, mistaking our part of the elephant and those negative emotions for reality—we just think we know better than everyone else.

This purely negative response, then, offers to solve the problem by pitting our personal perspectives against those of others. The worst part is that no one realizes it! We are living in an insane world in which everyone mistakes their own opinions, beliefs, and negative emotions for actual reality. We are already feeding the wrong wolf without knowledge or consent.

If this life-changing revelation falls a little flat for you, don't worry. We have all been trained to memorize and repeat the same mistakes our parents made, the ones their parents made, and on back through history. You will get it. I wish I could just give it to you by telling you, but you will eventually see it for yourself by living it, rather than just trying to understand a concept.

All change first begins with awareness.
—Anonymous

Until we are aware of the way things function, there is no possibility for change—but what we are doing right now, *this* is exciting! Right now, as you read this and relate it to your own life experiences, you are becoming aware! You are beginning to see the bars of your personal Matrix. What if all the things that are wrong in the world and in your life are just legless chickens fed by wrong-hearted wolves? Old, unexamined games of make-believe that others taught you to play in the past? We have all been quietly taught to try to make a dysfunctional, false reality function. But we can't see that yet because we've been immersed in that dysfunction since birth. We're like newly hatched fish: they don't know they are in water because they were born into it. They have never known anything else.

Beginning in early childhood, we experience being disowned or accepted through the approval and disapproval of others. They withhold love as a punishment, which none of us want to feel, and give love as a reward, something everyone wants to feel. This cycle has convinced everyone that this is the way our world works. Can you remember a time when a parent withheld love from you to punish you and then restored it as a reward when you behaved as they wanted? Have you withheld love from anyone as a punishment and given your love and affection as a reward? Where do you think you learned that?

Other people have been painting on our personal canvases since we were kids, but now imagine that they ran out of room. Instead of getting out a new canvas, they just kept painting around us, adding more layers, squeezing us into a tinier space. In time, we were surrounded by them on all sides, immersed in our own little world. Our personal Matrix.

Even though we were surrounded, people kept painting different interpretations of us and writing down their different requirements, expecting us to conform. Expectations, definitions, judgments, and labels. Be a good boy and do what you are told. Be a good girl and don't question your parents' authority. To be a "success," you'd better get into a good school, make a lot of money, forge a great relationship, and support your family. You have to make Mom and Dad proud, right? Doesn't the advice "make us proud" imply that they aren't already proud, and you must do something to earn it? If you want to do things to make them proud, you have probably played this I-am-not-good-enough game before.

Over the years, all those imagined versions of who we should be surround us until we have forgotten who we actually are. All around us is an imaginary world imposed upon us by others, enveloping us so completely that we believe this must be the entire world. This isn't just one part of the elephant; our perspective is the whole story, and all our rewards and punishments hinge on it. Anyone who says differently must be insane. They might even question the reality of Santa!

I made the same mistake. I was just an unrealized amalgamation of all those things that others decided I was while I was growing up. Quietly, over time, after so many punishments and rewards, I accepted it. I believed them. I eventually adopted those definitions as my personal Matrix of beliefs.

As you know, I didn't fare too well as a teen. I had reached my teen years bearing the pain of the misunderstandings and conditional love of my parents. Conditional love isn't actual love, it's conditioning. It's punishments and rewards to get a trained response, like training the family dog. Of course, it hurts.

I was dealing with my pain in a neglectful family by keeping my silence. I took on that family pet role, denying my emotional needs and staying out of the way. The funny thing about being defined by someone else or by a situation is that you have to choose to accept it. If you don't believe it, it has no effect. No one can make you feel like less without your consent. I did believe, after the diaper incident, that I was less than everyone else in the family. I was still sleeping on the floor in the living room, and I was just about to start high school. I didn't have my own bed, let alone my own room.

My brother had gotten his own room years earlier. I remember the all-day trip to go and have him pick out a bed, a dresser, and shelving.

It was a big family event. I was promised the same, but that never happened.

My dad was an amazing provider. He took us from lower middle class to solid middle class by the time I was 13, but there was no real depth to his relationship with me or my brother. So my brother acted out and I hit the gym.

Once I reached those teen years, I was fully prepared to resent my family for what I thought they had done to me. So many broken promises and so few times when they showed any kind of heartfelt care. Yes, today I fully and openly love my parents and they love me, but back then I loved them as conditionally as I believed they loved me. That never gave me the closeness I wanted.

My brother and I were both diagnosed at an early age with an eye disorder called retinitis pigmentosa. We were both destined to go blind, but the doctor said we would literally be in our 60s before it became an issue. I thought I had time to live a full life. All I had to do was finish high school and then get a college degree. I had no idea that the doctor was wrong.

High school isn't easy for anyone. So much is new in the teen years: the whole puberty thing, all the ways my body was changing, and those hormones. Nothing like throwing that into the Matrix mix for some extra confusion.

To make matters worse, my sight issues started hugely impacting every aspect of my life. I didn't want others to know that my sight was impaired. I also assumed that the doctor was right, so I didn't think I had to worry yet. I made many small mistakes, though, and that could make any simple situation, such as riding the bus to school, both logistically and emotionally complicated. It was the main consideration as far as what I chose to do and what I tried to avoid, in both my home life and my school life. There were plenty of clues that people could have seen if they'd been paying any attention.

The first indicator that someone has retinitis pigmentosa is night blindness. Since I was a little kid, I always wondered how other kids could play outside at night. For me, it was like being immersed in inky blackness. I could only see the streetlights and the circles they cast onto the road.

That was one reason that chasing my dad up the street at night was especially frightening for me. I could only see him when he entered and left the circle of light cast by each streetlight as he trudged away from the house. It was scary to be running as fast as I could to catch him, with no idea of what was in front of me.

THE HIGH SCHOOL YEARS

Every school day started by waiting for the school bus.

Finding a seat on the bus was rife with social politics. I didn't have any friends on my bus route, and even though each seat could accommodate two, those non-friends would sit in the outer seat, either to either reserve the inside seat for their friends who hadn't gotten on yet or to discourage others from sitting with them.

My vision complicated most things, but riding the bus was especially challenging. Throughout most of the darkest parts of winter, I had to guess which seats were open. I would try to make out the shape of a head in front of a window. Most times, I could see the silhouette of a person against the first light of early morning. That trick was the best idea that I had, and it had always worked.

One exceptionally dark morning, when I got on the bus I couldn't see a thing. There was no light in the sky at all. I looked for the silhouettes of seated students and saw nothing. The bus driver wasn't known for her patience, and her gruff grunting allowed for about 15 seconds until the bus lurched ahead again.

I had to hurry up and guess. I quickly assessed the row next to me. Seeing no outline against the dark window, I turned around and plopped into the seat—and landed squarely onto someone, who scrambled over to the other seat. I could tell that she was a girl from the perfume cloud she left in her wake and the girlish squeal she made as she tried to avoid my accidental attempt to sit in her lap.

I was mortified. I just froze like a statue. We spent the entire bus ride without a word. I still have no idea who I introduced my posterior to that day. Thanks, eyesight.

In general, I disliked high school. The stressed-out feeling I had all through grade school bled over into my high school years. My fear told me to avoid as many of the things that caused me stress as I could. As a result, I missed as many school days as possible.

When I did go, it was the same old thing. Memorize this. Take a test. Keep your head down and don't draw attention. If you memorize well, you get a good grade. If not, maybe you won't have a bright future.

I couldn't let anyone find out about my eyesight. Kids in school are brutal. Even among those I did hang out with, when I confided in them they would mess with me.

I never knew who was going to humiliate or endanger me—or when. It didn't happen all the time, and I never expected it when it did. Sometimes someone would turn out the lights, so that I couldn't see and they could. One time, when a group of us were driving to visit a friend, they let me out at a random house and left me there. Another time, someone pretended to be helpful by guiding me, then pushed me face-first into a tree. They liked to try to make me look ridiculous, like when I was dressed up to impress for a party and someone led me into knee-deep mud for a laugh. These were what my so-called "friends" did when I told them about my poor eyesight. I didn't want to find out what an enemy might do!

I skipped prom because my vision had already caused so many simple things to go embarrassingly wrong. I wasn't about to risk that potential disaster. Between my conclusion that I was no better than the family dog and the anxiety and logistics of my failing vision, I hid as much as I could.

What comes out when life squeezes you? When someone hurts or offends you?

> *If anger, pain and fear come out of you,*
> *it's because that's what's inside.*
> *—Wayne Dyer*

I survived high school by avoiding risky situations. There were so many things I didn't dare to participate in, so many girls that I hoped to get to know. So many parties that I didn't go to.

But my grades were good, and I was doing great at the gym. It turned out that I was unusually physically strong. I was very athletic but didn't play sports, again because of my eyesight. I was an all-star athlete growing up, but I would make occasional mistakes due to my vision that made me feel embarrassed. I would never do as well as I knew I could if I could see normally. I dealt with my life struggles at school and at home by hiding and denying all my emotional pain.

My brother struggled in his own way. The same dysfunctional household, along with the knowledge that one day he would go blind, drove him to lots of emotional issues. He acted out. This moved most of the small amount of attention that we both got to him—the squeaky wheel gets the grease. All his chores and responsibilities were added to mine, but he still got his allowance and my help was not acknowledged in any way. This filled me with resentment.

I was never a problem. I survived by not sharing my struggles. Because of all the things that happened during my childhood, I just didn't think the family could survive if I had any problems at all.

I was tricking myself, though. I did have problems. What are all problems made up of? The pain of negative emotions and the stories they generate. Thoughts and feelings. Can you ever have a problem that doesn't come from the path of negative emotions?

Do you ever complain about being loved too much or being too damn happy? Are you so full of peace that you can't help but complain to anyone who will listen? Me either.

I took my frustrations out at the gym, but I felt that there had to be something else. There had to be something that worked. In the very definition of dysfunction, there is implicit function. A way of doing things that doesn't suck. By this logic, I stumbled upon a great law of the universe: the law of contrast.

We can only experience things by contrast. We can't know healing without injury, or happiness without sadness. There would be no way for any learning or growth if we didn't have both limitations and the benefits that come from outgrowing them. How could we experience up without down or right without left? We need contrast to journey at all. That is the first gift of suffering. It is a pain signal trying to get our attention. It is an opportunity to stop and tend to the wound. To move from pain to healing.

We could never know function without dysfunction. We can't know true from false without both. The two paths are inherent in the design and expression of everything. We just mistake the limiting thoughts and emotions for the true path.

Throughout my childhood, I was afraid my family didn't love me. Since that is supposed to be a guarantee in every family, I thought that nobody else could either. If my family didn't, and they are required to, I thought I must be inherently unlovable. I was afraid I would never figure out how to earn anyone's love and no one would love me. I was even afraid of the dark.

In college, I met the other side of fear. I got angry. I was tired of fear telling me all the things that could go wrong or that I was the problem. Fear feels so disempowering. Anger felt better. It felt like power. I decided to take control and make everyone else the problem. It was a simple matter of judging them and making myself the giver of punishments and rewards. This was the perfect mistake, and it led me to do what I was about to do. I was about to get religious.

THE COLLEGE YEARS: FROM FEAR TO ANGER

I got into religion in college, partly because I was curious and partly because I was struggling some with my vision. I had spent my first two years at a local branch campus of Penn State University, but it was only a two-year school. There was only one local four-year college where I could get a degree.

My only commutable option was a Christian college. I wanted to find what most people are looking for when they turn to spirituality, the "truth that sets you free." That, to me, was what made the prospect of religion so attractive.

Religious people and institutions promise to have the answers for all of life's struggles. Not only do they claim to know the truth, they also say that what they believe holds the key to get into heaven. As long as you do what they tell you to, perhaps you will get there, too.

Wow! So, anyone can get free from suffering and get into heaven if they do what others tell them to do? Oh, I know this game! Conditional love rewards you for doing what people want, and punishes you when you don't. That is the same conditional love that my parents and teachers offered me.

This Christian college's brochure said that if you act now, heaven also comes with complete freedom from emotional suffering and a heart bursting with love! Quite the sales pitch, right? Who would say no to that?

What I was about to find at that college, however, was not the answer to anything, but the anger side of the dance of the legless chicken and the wrong-hearted wolf. Before I started down that anger path, however, something completely unexpected happened. I got a glimpse of the true path.

Just after I started classes, I began searching for that truth that would set me free. To my astonishment, I found something! What I found was indescribable. It was as if that shell that others had taught me to build around myself had been punctured by something greater. My limited, selfish perspective got a glimpse of the whole elephant. Something cracked open inside of me that didn't require belief. It was like one of those amazing rays of sunlight that breaks through a dark cloud. It was as if some deeper reality had gotten in, and I was connected to the bigger picture.

TRICKED AGAIN

I had discovered something truly magical, but I didn't understand it. I was new at this religion thing and had just started classes at this strange new Christian school, so I repeated the mistake that I had been taught. I started asking other students and teachers what they believed about what I had found. They all said that they knew the "right" way to do this religious thing, and that I was doing it "wrong." So, I deferred to them.

I got lots of input from students who had been religious their whole lives. I talked with professors of religious studies, and they told me all the right answers to give about all the questions I might consider or be asked.

Soon enough, I found that I had covered over the place where that shell had been pierced. I had spackled over it with beliefs. The "right" beliefs. Then I began to repeat the right answers that everyone else told me to say. The stale appearance of religion in place of the vibrant connection that I had glimpsed. I unwittingly fell back into my limited self-perspective.

I did exactly what we are all taught from birth: I went from connecting to a deeper, vibrant curiosity and aliveness to accepting the definitions of others and making them my own. Hoping to fit in and do it "right." Hoping that if I just redefined this greater reality according to what others told me, I would get the reward of heaven and avoid the punishments of hell. The desire to gain and the fear of loss. Again, the wrong damn wolf.

I forfeited my true-hearted connection to the aliveness that I'd discovered for the reward of being accepted as part of the club—the club of the self-proclaimed saved, who were making the same mistake that I was making now.

What happened in my childhood is that love and fear got flipped. We all start out as pure-hearted beings, full of curiosity and exuberance. We learn that we have to disown those qualities to meet the requirements of those around us. This has a universally tragic impact on our hearts and minds. We replace curiosity with conformity and true-hearted loving with the split between the fear of losing it and the strategy we can use to regain it. The pain of loss feels bad, and we want to feel good.

After this root violation of self-rejection, it is no longer okay to feel vibrant and alive. We are punished or rewarded to suppress our true heart, giving us the impression that it is the problem we must solve. In place of open, honest communication and trust with each person, we are taught to lie. To pretend to be who they want us to be, so we can earn or become worthy of love again.

> *Twixt hope and fear, anxiety and anger.*
> *—Horace*

Have you ever thought about why we lie? Don't we lie to gain some advantage or get what we want, or to avoid unwanted consequences? We only lie when we are afraid we will lose something, or in the hope of gaining something.

This is the duality of the wrong wolf. If lying is required of us to be acceptable to our parents, teachers, and friends, we are replacing the actual qualities of love—being patient and kind, the qualities of the good-hearted wolf—with the fear of being punished if we don't conform.

Didn't it feel good to get a reward when you were considered a "good" boy or girl? Didn't it feel bad when you were punished? Is doing something to avoid the pain of punishment or get a reward the same as doing that thing for the love of it? Can you see how the conditional love learned in childhood creates a cycle of fearing pain, simultaneously birthed with a desire to punish whoever we feel has hurt us?

We aren't who we think we are, or who we have been rewarded and punished to become. This won't be easy to see at first. For as long as we have been alive, everyone who has ever defined us has taught us through conditional love that the wrong path is the truth, and that has become part of our neurology.

What happens to our neurology when we feed one of the two wolves? It gets stronger. We build neurological connections. Which path do you think we are strengthening when at any moment, each different person can punish or reward us until we conform to their requirements to be a "good" or "bad" person in their eyes? Once we play the conditional love game and have fed that wrong neurology, the quiet baseline assumption that we are trained to make moves us internally from love to the threat response as our foundational constant.

That is where the universal problem is born. We mistake the thoughts and feelings from the Matrix of our negative limited selves for the truth of the entire world when it becomes the dominant path of our hardwired neurology. We believe that our way is the right way, and we go out into the world with the same attitude that we learned. People are right when they agree with us and wrong when they don't. It is exactly this dynamic that made for the perfect storm in my pursuit to make religion work at my Christian college.

THE WAKEUP CALL

'Tis with our judgments as our watches, none
Go just alike, yet each believes his own.
—Alexander Pope

I was early in my senior year and had spent my junior year getting to know some new people I thought were friends. Learning the strange new culture of the lifetime religious was awkward at first, but I had spent the first year learning the rules of conformity, and things had fallen into a rhythm of normality. The appearance of the routine norm can be deceiving, though. Habit can lull you into a false sense of certainty, believing that how things have been is how they will continue to be. Nothing had prepared me for what was coming.

My grades were solid. I had friends. Not the sort of friends that I was used to, but friends. And we were the "better" people. We had a shared morality. I had even risked sharing my depression and vulnerability with a trusted few.

I broke my high school rule. I revealed that I would go blind someday, as well as the pain that I constantly felt around the struggles with my sight. How the thought of losing it scared me and made me very depressed. Because I believed we were all God's special chosen ones, I was shocked when one person from the group I had shared this information with asked to talk privately with me. I was confused, because I had ticked all the required boxes.

I was like a boy scout's boy scout. I was following all the good people's rules. I didn't smoke, drink, swear, or have premarital sex. I memorized the right answers to religious questions and stayed awake through some impressively lifeless talks about eternal life. How was I not going to receive a good-person, God reward?

My friend said she wanted to talk to me about my sin. I had to ask what sin she was referring to. I didn't think I had committed any sins, but I wanted to know which one she was accusing me of. She answered, "What sin have you committed that God is punishing you for by taking your sight?"

I was stunned. Until then, I thought that all the good-person points were given based on how many good-boxes you ticked. Those were the rules, right? I had no idea that you could be punished for something you had no control over. I had been diagnosed with a genetic eye disorder when I was 4 years old. I couldn't imagine I had done anything before that age to warrant God punishing me by blinding me.

That was when I began to question everything they had told me about God, as well as my assumption that I was a part of their group. The group of the moral box-checkers.

There are two ways to be fooled. One way is to believe what isn't true; the other is to refuse to believe what is true.
—Soren Kierkegaard

When I joined that group, I believed that I was no longer one of those sinners, I was one of the special chosen. I was saved, like they were. We were all checking off those moral boxes, earning points to get into heaven. We were the "good" people.

By judging me as guilty and God as righteous for blinding me, this person denied me credit for all the good-boy, religious points I thought I'd been earning. It took me right back to all the arbitrary punishments of childhood. It seemed like no matter how many things I did right, none of it mattered. Someone else always had authority over me, which gave them the power of conditional love and arbitrary punishments.

One of the primary rules that I learned from my group was that God was the ultimate authority. He was the king of arbitrary punishments, and no matter what those punishments were, or how arbitrary, they were all because of his Love.

We, as the godly, were required to judge everyone on His behalf. We judged the people who didn't tick those boxes, because we were the box checkers. We were moral. Doing the moral things that allowed you to check those boxes inched you closer to the reward of heaven; being immoral, not meeting those requirements, brought each sinner closer to the fires of hell.

I'd done everything they taught me to do. I read and memorized what they put in front of me. I learned to judge others by their rights and wrongs, for not doing what I was doing. I even tried to stop listening to secular music in favor of some truly terrible alternatives. I did it all with the I-am-becoming-morally-better-than-other-people sense of self-satisfaction, like the rest of the group. I was doing everything they wanted. That always leads to rewards, right? Isn't that how you get into heaven?

Unbeknownst to me, all the thousands of times that I judged other people I was feeding the wrong path. I even thought it was a part of the spiritual practice. I thought that was how you became a better person. Maybe I was mistaking the dopamine hits and the adrenaline rushes for reality. Maybe I was mistaking the wrong-hearted wolf and legless chickens for the path of righteousness.

DECEIVED YET AGAIN

Remember how I fused the feeling of fear with the thought of public speaking, which created a fear of public speaking? I had made the same mistake based on a different negative emotion. I had become self-righteous. I really thought that I was becoming a spiritual person, but all the anger that fueled my punishing judgments was doing the exact opposite. Instead of becoming holy, I was becoming ass-holey.

I didn't realize that judging how things and people should be can only come from the path of the limited perspective and negative emotions. I was a legless chicken with a heart full of wrong wolf.

Have you ever heard the saying, "Opinions are like assholes, everyone has one"? I would expand on that to say that the more emotion we invest in our own opinions, the more we become like assholes. I certainly did. There are lots of great jokes about talking shit, but talk about being emotionally blinded to the truth of which wolf I was feeding and which path I was on! I had no idea that my personal Matrix was leading my religious self down the wrong path while calling it holy, and that due to my self-righteousness, no one was more ass-holey than I.

Early in college, I had found a genuine spirituality that I didn't create. I was full of love and humanity, and then I traded it for a caricature of God. The great, arbitrary punisher, whose any-and-all abuse was justified by calling it love. The same conditional love that I learned when I was young.

I didn't understand at the time the difference between belief and truth. Belief only comes from each person's limited perspective. It's personal and subjective. Truth is about function, not facts. The truth is in motion. Belief is an opinion frozen in time until tested or challenged.

Like gravity, truth functions the same for all of us. Go ahead and test that. See if gravity works differently for you based on what you believe about it or how you think it "should" work. Drop anything right now and see if it falls upward because you believe that it should. Unless you take gravity out of context—say, by going to outer space—it is an absolute truth in how it functions. When we mistake our personal beliefs for function, we are taking truth out of context, unknowingly replacing it with our limited perspectives.

It's funny now, and I thank that person for her question about my "sin"—because I was totally invested. I was building that negative neurology with every memorized verse, and it was a self-fulfilling prophecy because of those dopamine and adrenaline hits.

Dopamine is a pleasure chemical. The brain gets a dopamine hit when we get what we want. Anger gives a rush of adrenaline. That adrenaline rush I got when I vented my righteous anger or participated in a heated moral debate felt like power. Controlling who was rewarded for agreeing with me, and choosing the punishments for those who disagreed, felt "good."

This anger aspect of the wrong wolf was new to me. It wasn't fearful, it felt good. It told me that it was okay to judge people and hurt people. It told me that I was right, whereas fear had always told me that I was wrong. Anger gave me the self-righteous illusion that I knew the truth. That was enough to justify all the abuses.

MORE OF THE SAME

The people who ran the Christian school thought it was different from the secular schools because they used different language and labels, but it was still all about rewards for agreement and punishment for disagreeing. Nearly all the students had requirements before they would be friends with you. The first requirement was that you had to have the same religious beliefs. You had to be "saved."

If you were saved, they could treat you as a friend; if you weren't saved, you were a conversion project with friend potential: Conditional Love 101. The girls wouldn't even date the unconverted. The only difference I could see was that there were a ton more requirements to be met before you could ever accept yourself or be accepted by others, let alone be accepted by God. They took conditional love and the legless chickens of belief to a whole new level. And I bought into it, hard.

It was like with Santa but on steroids. I was going to get that reward of heaven and avoid the punishments of hell. I was going to outdo everyone else on that heavenly nice list. I adopted everything they taught me about God. I judged the hell out of everyone. I vented my "righteous" anger when people disagreed with me. Everyone had to earn my love, and I could remove it anytime I wanted to. Now I meted out the punishments and rewards as arbitrarily as I chose, just like their version of God.

When my friend told me to repent from the sin that caused God to blind me before age four, it woke me up to both her bullshit and my own. All that I learned was that whatever God's love was, the love that all my fellow box-checkers always talked about, it certainly wasn't this.

For a good part of my life, I struggled to understand the rules of the game, not realizing that I was learning them from the very people who were making them up. My parents, teachers, and friends were all the same. None of us had any understanding about function. All the systems and that I was exposed to were the same. Whether it was preacher, teacher, pauper, or king, they were all mistaking their personal perspectives for reality.

That is what made finding the real world so difficult. Everything that I was taught about the world, from the moment I was born, was based on that same mistake. Everyone was unknowingly trying to see the entire elephant based on their own limited piece of it. It was all situational ethics. No one taught me that there was any other option but to try to make my personal perspective the truth for the world, rather than finding that truth and aligning with it.

Because I adopted the anger aspect of the wrong-hearted wolf, I was never able to do the good I wanted to do; I only created more problems that were beyond my control. This hurt those that I cared about, instead of creating the love and family I felt I had lost.

My experiences at Christian school were similar to those I grew up with—the conditioned love from my family and my experiences of grade school, middle school, and high school. None of it worked, but I had done it. I had graduated from college with honors, and now my life could begin! Remember what I said about reality not necessarily caring a bunch about our plans? Well, I was about to learn that in screaming capital letters.

THE CHRISTMAS SURPRISE

I had my diploma and was finally about to begin the "good life." I was going to go out into the world and find that job, marry that girl, get that house, and have those two and a half kids. Freedom of conformity, hear me roar! A few things would get in the way that I didn't quite expect.

My vision wasn't doing so well. It varied from day to day, but I had been having a string of bad vision days. That seemed strange to me, because the doctors had said that I would have functional vision well into my 60s. I didn't even consider what was coming to be a possibility.

It was winter and, as I said before, I had always loved Christmas. What kid who still believed in Santa into his teens, and literally fought in Santa's corner, could say otherwise? I liked Christmas lights so much that I used to hang them around the borders of the ceiling in my bedroom. They were the last thing I saw before I fell asleep and the first thing I saw when I woke up. I always smiled when I saw those lights. I loved waking up to the sight of those bright, festive colors. It always gave me that sense of the magic of Christmas that I loved as a kid.

One day, about a week before Christmas, when I woke up I couldn't see my colored lights. I closed and opened my eyes a few times. I could see a glow, but not the lights. I tried stretching while squeezing my eyes shut and popping them open, but something was wrong. No matter what I did, I couldn't seem to see the lights. I felt panic rise up in me as I scanned the room and realized that overnight, I had lost the ability to focus. Overnight, I had gone blind.

I cried most of that day. I would never again see those Christmas lights that never failed to give me a smile and sparked that sense of child-like wonder.

Being blind was a whole new level of bad. I wasn't just feeling stressed or anxious. I would literally panic, and then I would pass out. I had no idea what to do—this wasn't supposed to happen, and it was terrible. In a single night, my life plans had changed.

I had struggled with depression all through school and college, but nothing had prepared me for this. This level of anxiety was different. It was overwhelming. It came out of nowhere and left me feeling helpless and hopeless. My friends, who had mostly moved on after college to start their lives, didn't stay in touch, and the few that I had contact with found reasons to avoid me. I remember one person's excuse about why we couldn't hang out anymore. "Sorry, man, but if people see you holding onto my arm in public, they might think we're gay."

My parents had no idea what to do either, but given the things they said, I knew I couldn't turn to them for support. Things like, "It's so sad. Your life is already over. You have no future. No one will want to be with you now that you are blind." And "What a shame. You were going to have such a good life, too." They said these things in an offhanded, wince-worthy way. The worst part was they actually seemed to believe my life was over. They weren't aware of how negative and limiting their judgments were before they spoke. My grandmother was in elder care at the time, and in a genuine moment of sorrow, despite the terrible panic and anxiety attacks I was having, I went to see her. She said, "Oh, my God! I am so sorry. I always told everyone that if I ever lost my sight, just kill me!"

What could I say to that but "Thanks, Grandma"? If only I had known then that she was just talking from her personal perspective. It actually had nothing to do with me. It was how limiting she imagined being blind would be and how she would feel if it happened to her.

THE DOWNWARD SPIRAL

I was lost. Overnight I literally went from sighted to blind and, in the ensuing weeks, to being jobless and friendless. I avoided my family, because they felt so bad that they only said terrible, depressing things about my life opportunities. Maybe I just heard things that way.

In my depression, I found that one thing hadn't changed: my appetite! I began eating like a vacuum cleaner with anger issues. I can remember that on many nights, my dinner would consist of a large pepperoni pizza, two orders of chicken strips with ranch dipping sauce, half a 2-liter bottle of soda, and yes, half a pie. And that was just dinner. Using this as my coping strategy, I got what some might call…fat.

I was pretty isolated and rarely saw any people or friends from the past—until a friend from high school came home to visit. I hadn't seen him in years. Everyone in my family was saying things like "It's not that bad, you look fine," and "You have all that muscle on you from working out, so you carry your weight well." When my friend Dan saw me, he chuckled and said, "Dude, you got fat!"

It's funny to think about that saying, "The truth hurts." I think it hurts more when someone is saying it due to negative emotions or trying to be hurtful. When Dan said it I felt ashamed for a second, and I remember looking down instinctively, but it was obvious that he wasn't trying to be mean. He was genuinely surprised. I felt a sense of gratitude that someone told me something true about myself that I suspected but hadn't really admitted.

The mix of emotions and my struggles with weight and blindness ate through the rest of my twenties. I was lost in a spiral of anxiety and depression, with no support and no understanding of what to do or how to reclaim my life.

Father, forgive them,
for they know not what they do.
—Jesus of Nazareth

The suffering produced by negative emotions is hidden and far extensive than we realize. It was fear that created all that anxiety from which I sought relief. I hated myself and the powerlessness that I felt. My anger fueled thoughts of using food as distraction from the emotional pain, and that cycle of fear triggering the pain and the resulting self-medication with food got me to tip the scales at over 300 pounds.

Don't all religions promise a loving God and access to the truth that will set us free? Why, then, did I continue to suffer? Why did nothing work? Why was all my life spent chasing my tail, chasing the idea of a freedom that was always promised but never came?

Because it's not possible. There is no freedom in the limited perspective, only the requirements of conditional love. When our freedom is contingent on gaining the approval of other people—or punishing or rewarding them so they can gain ours—it never works. It becomes a never-ending to-do list for us all. We'll never find true-hearted connection by forcing our demands on others or bowing to theirs. We can't punish our way to love or fear our way to trust.

That was my problem. For all my life so far, everything had come from the wrong path—the path of my limited perspective. I didn't realize it at the time, but I was making judgments and drawing conclusions about myself and other people. I believed my thoughts and emotions. I didn't realize that we have thoughts and we feel emotions. I was so deceived by the negative path that I believed the choices I made out of anger, fear, and sadness were the only choices that existed.

Like all the people I had met to that point, I was coming from my own limited perspective. None of us knew that we were interpreting reality through the lens of our personal matrixes, which is the level at which all problems are created. No matter how many times I followed the solutions generated by fear and anger, they always failed. Once I found the level where all problems are solved, that changed everything.

The path of actual Love always works, and the path of Fear and Anger always fails. The path of Love feels harder, though. Our true-heartedness feels like risk. Fear whispers the promise that it will keep us safe from loss by avoiding situations and Anger promises it will gain us what we want by controlling situations, but they both always come back to the punishments and rewards of conditional love. We have all mistaken the personal Matrix of what we believe for reality. The answer to the question "Why do I do the evil that I don't want to do, and not the good that I do want to do?" is simple. There is no way to make the path of dysfunction functional. No one can solve a problem from the same level that is creating it.

I finally discovered that I had mistaken the thing that was imprisoning me for the truth that would set me free. I discovered that for things to work, all I had to do was find the truth that already exists and simply align with it.

The Golden Rule: Universal Function versus Individual Belief
Act Three:
The transition to the path of reality

Words are not truth. Truth is like the moon, and words are like
my finger. I can point to the moon with my finger, but my finger
is not the moon. Do you need my finger to see the moon?
—Zen Master Hui-Neng

WHAT CAME FIRST, THE LEGLESS CHICKEN OR ITS EGG? Do you believe that your experience creates your perspective or that your perspective determines your experience?

If the path of negative emotions and the thoughts and stories generated by them can never lead to solutions but only more problems, what about the higher path? There can't be a path of pure dysfunction without a path of function, right?

Since the path of the negative-hearted wolf and the legless chicken is the path that creates our personal Matrixes—where all dysfunction is born—it is the level of the universal problem, where no solutions can be found.

The only way we will truly see any of this for ourselves in a life-changing way is not by believing or disbelieving in it, but by living it.

As Osho teaches: Thoughts are only fingers pointing at reality, they are not actual reality. All thoughts are made of words and all words are made up by someone. There is no reality in thoughts, they are only words. It all depends on how we use them and from which path.

Beliefs can be tricky because they take the words that make up thoughts and build them into stories, combining thoughts with emotions that make them feel real. Luckily for us, we can learn by contrast. There would be no way to recognize the true path without the false one.

The true path is the path of wisdom. The path of direct, personal experience in real time, in the present moment, in which we can observe, learn, and live in alignment with what is true.

Being present in the waves of thoughts and emotions, so that we can ride the wave instead of reacting, judging, or defining it. Can you catch the wave if you aren't there when it comes up? Can you learn to surf the waves by believing things about surfing instead of actually surfing?

Until now, we have seen the two paths in different ways. Now, we have the dynamics of both paths represented by contrasting the stories and beliefs and their emotions, as well as the path of function. We could even make an equation to this point for function and dysfunction. A simple equation for the misapplied fight-or-flight path is: Threat limits Choice, creating Inequality.

The higher path of the good wolf is simply restoring balance to a nervous system that is distorted by the fight-or-flight response. That equation could be summed up as: Reduction of the Threat response through relaxation, the resulting expansion of Choice, and the restoration of Equality.

Remember, there is solid science showing what happens every time the fight-or-flight neurology is triggered. The blood in the area of the brain where our decisions are made is reallocated to the muscles to prepare to fight—or flee, if necessary. Our good decision–making center is impaired to the degree that we react, because the blood required to keep that area functioning properly is gone. So, there is even physiology behind the bad decisions encouraged by the wrong path.

THE UPSIDE DOWN

Fear, anger, and sadness come from the limited personal-perspective promise that if we follow their advice, our unkindness will make us kind. That our fear will protect us. That quitting will solve the struggle. Our worry and our hurry will save time or make us better people.

All the while, it degrades and harms us, and we then harm those around us. We have less time, less patience, less kindness to share and no peace of mind by which to see our mistake. The world is turned upside down, calling evil good and good evil.

This is what all the wisdom teachers have been showing us for thousands of years: the function of things and not the judgments. They realized the one problem that we all suffer from: we have mistaken our limited perspective for truth, and we have combined it with the wrong-hearted wolf, which says that the "good" sensations of getting what we want and the "bad" emotions when we don't get what we want are actually good and evil.

THE TRUE PATH: THE PATH OF LOVE

"If I speak in the tongues of men or of angels, but do not have Love, I am only a resounding gong or a clanging cymbal. If I have the gift of prophecy and can fathom all mysteries and all knowledge, and if I have a faith that can move mountains, but do not have Love, I am nothing. If I give all I possess to the poor and give over my body to hardship that I may boast, but do not have Love, I gain nothing.

"Love is patient, Love is kind. It does not envy, it does not boast, it is not proud. It does not dishonor others, it is not self-seeking, it is not easily angered, it keeps no record of wrongs.

"Love does not delight in evil but rejoices with the truth. It always protects, always trusts, always hopes, always perseveres.

"Love never fails. But where there are prophecies, they will cease; where there are tongues, they will be stilled; where there is knowledge, it will pass away. For we know in part and we prophecy in part, but when completeness comes, what is in part disappears.

"When I was a child, I talked like a child, I thought like a child, I reasoned like a child. When I became a man, I put the ways of childhood behind me.

"For now we see only a reflection as in a mirror; then we shall see face to face. Now I know in part; then I shall know fully, even as I am fully known.

"And now these three remain: Faith, Hope, and Love. But the greatest of these is Love."

The above text from 1 Corinthians 13 is part of the Christian tradition. It is one of the most widely known and accepted writings on love. It is a beautiful expression of the two paths.

The natures of the two paths are expressed in two ways. The path of love unifies. It brings a sense of oneness and understanding. The survival path of the fight-or-flight nature splits everything into the duality of the desire to gain and the fear of loss. Both the desire to gain and the fear of loss split into a never-ending division of "dos" and "don'ts," "shoulds" and "shouldn'ts," "coulds" and "couldn'ts."

Love is patient and kind. When negativity is stirred, awakening our survival nature, are we patient or impatient? Are we kind or abusive? This survival nature always wants to hide. The very function of flight is to run and hide; the very function of fight is to control. To be threatened or be the one making the threats. The one who is in control or the one who is controlled. The predator or the prey.

When a situation arises that goes against what you think the world should be, what are the two courses of action recommended by this nature? You can either make it "right" by taking control of the situation and defining it in terms of how you think things should be, or—if you are too afraid—you can allow others, or the situation, to define you. You can be the wolf or the sheep: Take control or avoid being punished. Do whatever needs to be done to achieve the goal. Get what you want through defining the world in your own image and avoid the pain of consequence when it creates more dysfunction.

All those thoughts that flood through us when we have negative emotions can never achieve the true-hearted intention that we all have. All Truth, with a capital T, comes from the true-hearted path of Love and the true-minded perspective of the whole.

Love, peace, and joy and fear, anger, and sadness are the two paths of the heart—the two wolves—and they are being fed by us, moment by moment, in every moment that we are alive.

Also, the two paths of the mind—the personal, limited perspective and the perspective of the whole, which is the path of true function—are always available to us, depending on which emotions we feed by focusing on them. Exactly like what happened in the relationship between me and my brother.

> *He who cannot forgive breaks the bridge*
> *over which he himself must pass.*
> *—George Herbert*

After I graduated from college and lost my sight, my brother and I had been estranged for a long time. I hadn't spoken to him in years. The drama of his acting out and all his struggles had deprived me of my parents' attention for most of my childhood and teen years. I had taken on all his responsibilities, but he'd been rewarded for them because my parents didn't want to make him more upset.

He called one day to talk with my mom. I was in my late 20s, living in my parents' basement and struggling with my blindness. My mom called down the stairs and said that my brother wanted to talk to me; he was asking for forgiveness. That he was sorry he'd taken all the attention, and he realized that he had left me without much of a childhood.

I had had enough at that point. I was angry, and I credited myself with carrying all that pain for my dysfunctional family through all those years. I thought I was the good guy, making up for their failures. Now, my brother was asking me to do what an actual good guy would do. I looked inside, and I could not forgive him. I told him that if I let that grudge go, all that suffering would mean nothing—so no, I would not forgive him. The resentment was all that was left from that childhood of neglect.

This went on for years. I would think about how to get back at my brother for the pain I felt by finding some way to get in a good shot. To find some point of weakness in him and exploit it. I was on the wrong path, telling myself that I had good reasons to justify feeding the wrong wolf.

It was long after I started exploring and understanding the dynamics I am sharing with you that something magical happened: I had a dream.

I dreamed that I had just gotten one over on my brother. A really good FUCK YOU! I was relishing the feeling, even while a part of me knew that he would come back at me. I had won this round, though, and this feeling of putting him down and putting myself above him, which at the time I thought was "winning," felt good.

The dream shifted, as dreams do, to a moment when I was in my bedroom. I was exhausted and defenseless. I was crawling into bed, and then my door opened. There he was. My brother was going to get back at me. I looked into his eyes and for the first time, I realized that he wasn't there to get back at me—he was going to kill me. With his right hand pulled back to conceal whatever weapon he had, he moved toward me without a single word. The hatred in his eyes said everything.

An unexpected playfulness bubbled up in me at that moment. I leaped up out of bed and, laughing, met him halfway into the room and jumped on him. We both fell onto the bed. He was caught by surprise. He was struggling to get some blows in, but couldn't reach the weapon. Suddenly, we both turned back into little kids, laughing and wrestling on the bed. I said, "I love you, Jeffy." And I woke up.

In that moment I saw the whole dynamic at once. The whole of the elephant. I saw that I only ever wanted to keep hurting him to make sure he would come back to me for a chance to reconcile. The path of dysfunction had me trying to reconnect by disconnecting. All that time spent in those negative cycles of conflict could never get us to reconciliation. There is no way to solve a problem from the level that is creating it.

For 20 years, I tried to get the better of him and the negativity got the better of me. All the thoughts, words, and actions I had invested were only escalating the negativity until we either broke contact permanently or it escalated into violence. The solution came from the other level that doesn't create problems: it came from the path of forgiveness.

I emailed my brother the details of the dream, and we started talking. We reconciled, and I was able to forgive him and let go of the burden I'd carried around from childhood. Forgiveness, like all the unifying qualities from the true path, unites. It benefits both.

In forgiving him, I set down the burden of the grudge I'd carried. He got to let go of his guilt. Mine was the burden of blame, and I was able to forgive myself, too, for all the things I had done to him.

I didn't have to continue the pattern of making him the perpetrator, me the victim, my beliefs the judge and jury, and my own negativity the executioner. You can't fight your way to peace. You can only realize that fighting can never get you there and decide to make peace.

When something goes "wrong" and we react negatively, we lose touch with who we truly are. We are reduced to a much smaller, petty version. Each time we are negative, we become a caricature of ourselves and humanity. This selfish, limited nature, however, is the lie that can help to show us the truth that will set us free.

What we need to realize right now is that every time this fight-or-flight response is triggered, it is the limited, fearful self. It springs from being rejected as children. The belief that we have to become something else to be acceptable to others, or to make others unacceptable until they conform to us.

The natures of the two paths are expressed simply by humanity and inhumanity. Love and conditional love. Truth is universal. That doesn't mean everyone has to believe the same thing; it means that it works the same for everyone. Its function of it is universal, like the function of gravity. Actual Love brings oneness because it is the Truth of actual function. When it is lived, it benefits all.

Reread those verses from 1 Corinthians. They are all just a comparison of the two paths of the heart and mind. They start with all the wrong wolf expressions of false love: The way it can attempt to be faked. The way the limited perspective of the petty "little i" self is always trying to convince us that it is really the good path.

Let's translate some of these verses in terms of the two paths.

"If I speak in the tongues of men or of angels, but do not have Love, I am a resounding gong or a clanging cymbal." Well, if you know the right things to say so that you appear to be a good person to those around you, to get what you want from them, it's not about loving them, it's only about you. Love as a pretense is the appearance of love, but it is empty. It never builds real trust.

"If I have the gift of prophecy and can fathom all mysteries and all knowledge, and if I have a faith that can move mountains, but do not have Love, I am nothing."

No matter your education or skill or money or level of accomplishment, if you are not connecting to your true heart you're just coming from the selfish perspective. It will never have a meaningful impact.

"If I give all I possess to the poor and give over my body to hardship that I may boast, but do not have Love, I gain nothing."

This is straight out of the desire to gain and the fear of loss. If you do anything falsely, motivated by gain or fear of loss, you truly gain nothing.

What does it feel like when you give out of a true sense of kinship or open-heartedness without asking anything in return? It's not the standard transaction of "you give me what I want, and I will give you what you want" from the wrong path; it's a gift given freely without requirements or agenda.

Then, the verse goes into a direct contrast of the two paths. A straight up comparison of good wolf and bad wolf.

"Love is patient, love is kind. It does not envy, it does not boast, it is not proud. It does not dishonor others, it is not self-seeking, it is not easily angered, it keeps no record of wrongs. Love does not delight in evil but rejoices with the Truth. It always protects, always trusts, always hopes, always perseveres."

Next, the verse does the most amazing thing! It compares belief with function. It compares the "little i" perspective of the parable of the three blind men and the elephant with the wholeness perspective of truth.

"Love never fails. But where there are prophecies, they will cease; where there are tongues, they will be stilled; where there is knowledge, it will pass away. For we know in part and we prophecy in part, but when completeness comes, what is in part disappears.

"When I was a child, I talked like a child, I thought like a child, I reasoned like a child. When I became a man, I put the ways of childhood behind me.

"For now we see only a reflection as in a mirror; then we shall see face to face. Now I know in part; then I shall know fully, even as I am fully known."

It's the comparison of the limited perspective to the whole! To me, the most powerful line in the whole writing is right there. "Love never fails. But where there are prophecies, they will cease; where there are tongues, they shall be stilled."

What is belief creation but words? What is prophecy but people predicting an unknowable future based on their beliefs? What if love can never actually fail, and the only time it can appear to fail is when we try to replace its universal function with our limited perspective? Shouldn't the limited perspective be sacrificed for the higher spiritual path, replacing selfishness with selflessness?

Since we have all been taught the mistake of trying to make the limited perspective the whole, we have been taught to focus on thinking in place of function. For thousands of years, the world has been looking to people for a belief or set of beliefs that will work. We had forgotten that the only things that function are truths.

For our whole lives, we have been taught to believe. To believe in who we think we are and how we think the world should be. But belief isn't living. It's thinking about living.

The verse ends as beautifully as it began, showing the three main qualities of the true-hearted path by saying: "And now these three remain: faith, hope, and love. But the greatest of these is love." If the false trinity from the wrong wolf is fear, anger, and sadness, the real trinity is love, peace, and joy. Is faith not peaceful?

Is hope not the anticipation of joy?

THE HIDDEN ENEMY

All those qualities give us a glimpse into love, but what, then, is evil? If love is patient and kind, caring and sharing, what are some of the expressions of evil? In religious terms, the term "sin" is used. Translated directly from the original Greek, it means to miss the mark. To misunderstand. To mistake the false path of the limited, selfish perspective for the truth, as well as mistaking the path of problems for the level of solutions.

What commonalities do all evil acts share? Whether devil or dictator, what do they have in common? The emotions of the Threat response. Anger and Fear on a scale. What emotions motivate all evil actions? When we think about our archetypes for evil, we usually think of demons and devils. If we just use Satan as the ultimate example, he is often called the father of lies. Don't we lie when we fear consequences or manipulate others so that we can get what we want? We lie to avoid taking responsibility and to avoid punishment. We also lie in hopes of gain.

Child or CEO, both lie to avoid being held responsible for their actions when they think there will be consequences, and they will say anything if they think they can profit. If they are given power over others, they will abuse others to get what they want. The soft lie or the crack of the whip.

What emotions do the demons and devils delight in? Are they hateful, fearful, selfless, or selfish? The emotions of evil are anger and fear on a scale. Lies to avoid a consequence or gain advantage and threats to do the same. The fear of personal loss combined with the desire for personal gain. If you do not have love, you have nothing.

In contrast to the good-hearted wolf, the wrong wolf comes up each time we don't get what we want. In the blink of an eye, we are making everything about us! We feel that emotional reaction come up in the moment, judge it as right or wrong or good or bad based on our personal perspectives and not true good or evil. We make it about us.

When we don't get what we want, we get upset. When we are frustrated, worried, feeling pressured, or insulted—or feel any of the countless expressions of negativity—the fight-or-flight response is the reaction. The fight-or-flight response is a universally true indicator of when we fall into the limited perspective. Can anyone judge anyone, or anything, without making it about themselves? The negative emotions and externalizations, projected onto others, are just a way of distracting us from the fact that we are creating the judgments. We aren't part of the whole of the world; we are trying to remake it in our own image. We are thinking that person should be like us. Just like our parents and peers did to us as children.

What else is anyone saying when they judge something, other than "Everything is about me. The world and all the people in it should only be how I want them to be, and never give me what I don't want. Look and act like I want you to, and I will reward or punish you according to the degree to which you comply." Is this not acting like a spoiled child?

We react because our expectations of how things should be are violated by how they are. How could anyone, you or I, ever react negatively to anything unless we already had an idea of how things should be?

How dare that person say or do what they said or did! I am a good person! How awful that I spilled my coffee on my new clothes. Stupid! How dare that chubby man in the very back of the theater do whatever he was doing to those poor penguins! Any number of events can upset us, and instead of realizing that our negative reaction is a blaring sign that we have mistaken our personal beliefs for the truth in the moment, we are washed away by it and replaced by a version of ourselves that is much dumber, deceived into thinking that our angers, our fears, our worries and abuses are not the very same qualities that those demons or devils possess. In truth, they are all justified by the very nature of evil itself.

ALL PERSONAL PERSPECTIVES ARE LIMITED

While I was attending that Christian school, I told people I thought were friends that I was blind. They judged me for it. I didn't share any of the diagnosis or details in high school except with a very few friends who saw that something wasn't working right with me at times. I would drop a pen or pencil and couldn't find it on the floor. I would sometimes misjudge something and walk into a doorway or something else I didn't see.

When I shared my blindness with those few in my circle of friends, each reacted and judged from their personal beliefs. Some pitied me. Others tried to imagine what it would be like if they went blind and how it would ruin their lives, and then assumed that it would limit or ruin my life.

For their own amusement, others that called themselves my friends led me face first into trees and tried to convince me to jump over non-existent streams. Not one of us, including myself, realized that the things they thought and imagined weren't actually about me, but reflected their personal views of the world. They were making judgments and drawing conclusions based on their personal perspectives.

At the Christian college, other students tried to get me to repent. They told me it was their Christian duty to explain that it was my sin that God was punishing. God was just their excuse to abuse, to judge—not according to any higher truth, but according to their personal interpretations—and call it truth. They said I deserved it and needed to examine all my sins, beg forgiveness, and repent.

No one, no matter how judgmental, cruel, or abusive, ever thinks—even for a second—that they are the bad guy. I certainly didn't, even though I was doing the exact same things at that Christian college. None of the people who did those things to me realized that each abuse was motivated by negative emotions and that they were judging based on their limited perspectives, and neither did I.

After a lifetime of confusion and way more abuses than I could ever list here, of course things got worse. Just after graduating from college—remember where I was in my struggles? I was deep into my darkest hours. I weighed over 300 pounds, and I couldn't leave the house due to my panic attacks. I was severely depressed and the pain of all this negativity and seeing no way out made me feel hopeless. There was so much pain that I wanted to die. I had not yet realized it at the time, but no one really wants to die; we just want the pain to end. But don't know how to end it.

I felt no control over my life at all. I couldn't even take comfort in the idea of a loving God. All I had ever known in my life was that even the smallest kindness had to be earned, and that arbitrary punishments could be justified by anyone at any moment, even if you never did anything wrong. This is also when I believed that other people's opinions were truths. None of it was true, and none of it was love. I had no way to know and no way to tell.

THE GOLDEN RULE: THE UNIVERSAL MEASURE OF THE TWO PATHS OF HEART AND MIND

Wouldn't it help to have a universal measure to instantly tell the difference between the deceptive false path and true humanity? A friend of mine asked me a great question: if everyone is unknowingly living from their opinions, how can anyone ever find the truth?

A standardized, conceptual answer from philosophy might go like this: The limited perspective is subject to the viewpoint of that individual alone, and is therefore what is called subjective, whereas a universal point of view maintains absolute objectivity. No bias or agenda. It's an objective, functional tool and no one's opinion.

We have all been very close to this discovery for a long time, but because we have been taught that every search ends when we define something or accept someone else's definitions as true, we haven't been able to find it. We stopped at definition without getting to function. We were taught to memorize and were rewarded or punished based on our answers. We made it into a static, unexamined belief. A brand-new legless chicken is born into the world!

After all, we are taught that that's what learning is. We have lost the reality that truth is function—the real-time function of heart and mind.

Initially, all that we can do is notice the differences between the two paths. After that, the Golden Rule offers an instantaneous, split-second indicator of which path anyone is on. It doesn't matter how rich, poor, self-important, or unimportant people believe themselves to be. Belief, and even facts, are not required to find true function.

As opposed to basing things on the judgments and conclusions of oneself or others, both the Golden Rule and the dynamics of threat—with its limiting effect on free will and the inevitable violation of equality—are objective measures. The functional aspect of Truth is always objective in the same way that opinions and perspectives are always limited to the person holding them. The issue arises when the negative nature turns reality upside down, telling us to impose our opinions on the world and others at the expense of the whole of the truth. Replacing the reality of the whole elephant with an individual's limited experience of one piece of the elephant.

Truth is always objective. No one can own it or define it. Like gravity and unconditional love, it is simply experienced directly by each person. It cannot be expressed through words alone. Words can only draw a bullseye around Truth, pointing to it so that we might hit the mark. Words are fingers pointing at the moon; they are not the moon. Each person must try as many times as they need to, until they hit the target.

LET'S LOOK AT THE EXPRESSIONS OF THE GOLDEN RULE FROM DIFFERENT WISDOM TRADITIONS.

1. In the Talmud of the Jewish tradition, the sage Hillel said: "What is hateful to you, do not do to others. This is the whole of the Law; all the rest is commentary."

2. In the Hindu legend of the Mahabharata, the divine Krishna declared: "This is the sum of duty. Do nothing unto others which would cause you pain if done to you."

3. In the Gospel of Matthew in the Christian scriptures, the messiah Jesus says: "Whatever you wish that others would do to you, do also to them, for this is the Law and the Prophets."

4. In the Buddhist text of the Udanavarga, the student is urged: "Hurt not others in ways that you yourself would find hurtful."

5. In the Muslim Hadith of al Nawawi, the prophet Mohammed teaches: "No one of you is a believer until he desires for his brother that which he desires for himself."

6. In the T'ai Shang treatise of Taoism, the seeker is instructed: "Regard your neighbor's gain as your own gain, and your neighbor's loss as your own loss."

7. In the ancient wisdom of Shinto, there is a saying: "The heart of the person before you is a mirror. See there your own form."

The Oglala Lakota spiritual leader Black Elk wrote: "All things are our relatives; what we do to everything, we do to ourselves."

THE ROOT VIOLATION: THE IMPOSITION OF WILL

Do not judge, or you too will be judged. For in the
same way you judge others, you will be judged, and
with the measure you use, it will be measured to you.
—Book of Matthew 7:1

Given all the variations of the Golden Rule stated above, what must be done to honor it and how is it violated? We must do unto others as we would have done unto us, and not do to others what we would not want done to us.

What root action is always taken to violate the Golden Rule? The imposition of will, of one's limited personal perspective, onto another.

What happens every time we judge ourselves or others in thought, word, or action? What about verbal abuse or physical violence? What are we doing when we lie to hide the truth? We are trying to remake the world in our image. They are all examples of the imposition of will.

Which emotions make people hide their intentions and manipulate others? What emotions turn people to violence? Anger and fear. They are a corruption of both heart and mind. The wrong path, imposing its definitions of how things should be onto others. Trying to prove to itself and the world that it isn't the limited, selfish perspective, full of negative emotions, but the whole of how things are and how they should be.

You may not realize it yet, but any time you have ever imposed your will on anyone in thought, word, or action, you have committed an act of violence. When others have done that to you, it was an act of violence. When you have done that to yourself, it was an act of violence.

When people don't judge and define, criticize, or compare, when they treat each other as equals, the Golden Rule is honored, and it feeds a greater humanity.

This is all that is needed to measure every situation and instantly shows when thoughts, words, and actions are in alignment with truth and love and when they stem from the fear of loss and the desire to gain. It is the measure of function.

No violation or violence can happen when the Golden Rule is honored. If no one is imposing their will, how can we harm anyone else or ourselves? The Golden Rule can never fail to function. Love and the perspective of the whole never fails. The only time things fail is when someone is imposing their will on us or we draw on our limited perspectives to impose our rules on others and the world.

MY WILL (AND NOT *THY* WILL) BE DONE

Simone Biles is the greatest gymnast of all time. In the 2021 Summer Olympics, she dropped out of most of the events that she had dominated for years to preserve her mental health and physical safety.

The expectations put upon her were the centerpiece of the entire Olympic games. She was the poster child for perfection. It was all over the news.

I was talking to someone who believed that it was wrong of Biles to drop out. He asked me if I agreed or disagreed with him. If I affirmed this limited perspective, judging it as "true," he would, in turn, affirm me as being "right" like him. If I disagreed, I would be denying his beliefs, and that negative emotion would be enough to justify punishing me by judging me as "wrong." On the false path, everything is about punishments and rewards.

In this instance I didn't get washed away by my emotions, and I was able to take the path of the wise man in the story from Chapter 2.

Curiosity without conclusion. Instead of agreeing or disagreeing with him from my limited perspective, I asked honest, curious questions.

First I asked him why Biles's non-participation was important to him. The path of the limited perspective always needs to be right, or make someone wrong, to maintain the illusion that it alone knows the whole of the Truth.

I neither agreed nor disagreed, and that makes the limited perspective want even more to be right, to make others wrong. My friend didn't answer the question. He asked me if I was one of those people who believed that everyone should get a trophy, even if they finish last. Was I one of those people who believed in self-esteem without merit?

That would have been a good question if I were arguing for anything, but the perspective of the whole doesn't need to argue, because it doesn't take sides. It realizes that all chosen sides come from the limited perspective of the one choosing them. It's not about a "right" or "wrong" opinion, it's about function.

For the person asking these questions, it was only about him and his limited perspective. It's a lose/lose conversation if we choose sides. Whenever people are talking from their limited perspectives, they are all looking to affirm or deny their own beliefs. Being affirmed feels good—we get acceptance and agreement. To disagree only results in conflict. But when two limited perspectives argue about which one is truth, both opinions are coming from limited perspectives. We are asking them to walk a mile in our shoes, instead of walking a mile in theirs.

I asked him how Simone Biles's personal decision affected him. He asked me if I was a socialist.

Dealing with people who are totally lost in attempting to make their personal point of view into the worldview of everyone around them isn't right or wrong. It's the way we mistake our limited, personal perspectives for truth. Whether you affirm or denigrate someone's opinion, it doesn't serve anything but greater dysfunction, believing that the personal perspective—ours or theirs—is the truth of the whole.

Here is the entire trick of the wrong path in a nutshell. When we are thinking about something and have emotional reactions to the thoughts, we then draw conclusions based on whether it feels good or bad, and that makes us believe that thoughts plus feelings equal reality!

All perspectives are unique to the person holding them, yet we believe—and that word is intentional—that just by the smallest piece of information, we can judge anything and everything. Oh, it doesn't feel like it is coming from the petty bias of our limited perspective. It feels true, so it is true.

We feel like we have made it true by judging it to be true. Our personal conclusion "feels" true, and we don't realize it's just another legless chicken. We are deceived by a dopamine hit, powered by negative emotions born from our limited perspective.

TO MAKE ANYTHING WORK, HONOR THE GOLDEN RULE

It is totally fine to have personal preferences. If you can accept that, then you can allow everyone to have their limited, personal perspective without the need to try to make them agree with yours, or you with theirs. No one defines anyone in their image.

When we were children, how did conditional love function? We were considered good or bad based on the limited perspectives of whoever was judging us. We were trained with punishments and rewards and taught that it was our exuberance that was the problem. It became a negotiation of self-suppression to meet the requirements of others. Situational ethics based on each person and circumstance.

We are born into a reality of wonder and curiosity, which is quickly replaced by a Matrix that was imposed on us. Ultimately, we believed this to be who we are and how the world is, but this isn't our journey. It's a piecemeal quilt made of what other people have rewarded and punished us to become. A self-portrait painted by others, bearing our forged signature.

We all dream of freedom, but we have forgotten from what. As children, we had to meet dozens or even hundreds of requirements to be loved. That is the burden we all feel when we hold ourselves to the impossible standard of the false path of conditional love.

It's exhausting and discouraging. It's a perpetual to-do list that never ends. It's the dysfunction that we can't make function. What we are realizing now is that it all comes from our limited perspective and the limited perspectives of others.

If you are not imposing your perspective on anyone and no one is imposing theirs on you, is that not freedom? Is that not how functional truth will set you free? The only limits that you will feel are what you have been conditioned to be in the past.

BECOMING THE CHANGE

We can't see that we are stuck in the limited perspective. Do you think the rule that says everything and everyone is equal, with the same rights and opportunities and free-will choice, everyone free from the imposition of the will of others, is a smaller or bigger perspective?

Is it seeing the pieces of the elephant or the entirety of the animal? Is it based on what you or I like? Do you think that if we agree or don't agree with something or someone, we are judging from our personal preferences and limited perspectives? Or is our individual belief supposed to rule the world?

If the path of love and the honoring of all individual perspectives equally is the higher path, taught by all the wisdom teachers, don't all solutions come from the path of function? We are so asleep to reality because of the beliefs that shroud it that we literally cannot tell darkness from light. That is what the spiritual teachers came to show us. The path of dysfunction can never function.

How often do you hear people who are unwittingly immersed in the negative nature say that the idea of humanity can't happen? That those who hold power will never let it go and the world will remain as it always has been? I would ask those people to find me one dark room that extinguished a candle, or one dark night that defied the light of dawn.

Darkness can only whisper fear in the shadows. It can only tell us that the possibility to change is the lie. That things are hopeless and things will never work. In reality, change is the only constant. Darkness is destined to fail.

The simple dynamic of the imposition of will and the path of the true heart shows us both when and how to light up the darkness.

We all fell into the darkness of our personal Matrices as children. We were separated from our true hearts and minds. We lost touch with our true purpose and genuine journey. Now, we understand the two paths.

Do not impose your will onto anyone and do not accept anyone's will imposed onto you. Own your life and no one else's. Take back your power to choose from all who have defined it in the past. Move forward into something new. Reclaim the power of your life, freely chosen in alignment with your vibrant, true, loving heart!

Taking Back the Journey
Act Four: Aligning with reality

With great responsibility comes
the imposition of will.
—Steven Fidler

PLATO'S *ALLEGORY OF THE CAVE*

IN PLATO'S *ALLEGORY OF THE CAVE*, Socrates describes a group of people who have spent their entire lives chained to a blank wall. These people watch shadows projected onto the wall by objects passing in front of a fire and give those shadow objects definitions. The prisoners come to believe that the shadows are reality.

It is then explained that a seeker of wisdom is like a prisoner freed from chains. He comes to realize that the shadows on the wall of the cave are not reality at all. They are a false reality created by mistaking the limited, personal perspective of defining and believing for reality. Once they understand this they can perceive reality's true form, rather than the manufactured reality of the shadows seen and defined by the prisoners.

For the most part, the inmates of this place do not even desire to leave their prison. They have no idea that there is a truth beyond their definition. If anyone challenges the way they have defined and explained this shadow reality, they can become confused or upset. Despite this, one day the prisoners manage to break their bonds and discover that their reality was not what they had imagined it to be. They also discover the sun.

Just like the fire that was behind them, casting shadows, the sun symbolizes the fact that the human condition is forever bound to the senses and the definitions we give those shadows, even if they are totally inaccurate.

How can we begin to free ourselves from the habit of judging and defining the world in our own image, unless we first realize that we are the ones naming the shadows? If we do manage to break these bonds, we can discover a world that we have not yet seen. A higher reality beyond believing or disbelieving. It is the realm of pure form and function, the realm of Truth.

What if we, like the prisoners, are all making that same mistake? What if we are mistaking the path of "thoughts plus feels equals totally for reals" for the whole of reality? How then, can we tell the difference between our beliefs and what is true?

Santa is one of my favorite examples. Did believing in Santa make Santa true, just because you or I believed? Or is reality totally independent of our definitions and conclusions?

How could we possibly make that mistake unless we deceived ourselves by naming those shadows on our cave walls and mistaking the feelings in the emotions that we invested in for reality? What about truth, then? Is truth the same as just believing or disbelieving something? Think back to my experience with Nick. Was it simply believing or not believing that showed me Santa wasn't real, or did I have to examine my assumptions after Nick challenged them? It didn't seem to matter whether I believed or not. Since I couldn't find truth by believing or disbelieving in something, I had to look at what was really going on. It took a long time, but I finally realized that truth is found through the patterns of direct, self-evident experience.

For those of us who are still mistaking the shadows on the walls of our caves for reality, isn't it the simple difference between the two paths, with personal perception being the individual limited perspective and reality being the truth of the whole?

With Santa, and all beliefs, it may very well be the case that perception is the individual perspective of the limited self, while reality is the way things actually are. Perception is individual and reality is universal.

If the difference between believing a thing and observing a thing without defining it, in real time, is the key factor in realizing the difference between our limited, personal perspectives and the real-time functioning of reality, we can't stop at conclusions; we need experiences.

It's just like the difference between reading the menu at a restaurant and tasting the food. Imagine being satisfied with reading the descriptions on a menu, judging what we believe we will like and won't like, instead of tasting the food and learning what we do like.

Regardless of what we believe or imagine about the experience from reading the menu, we have no actual information until we taste the food. What if we just read the descriptions on the menu and never actually tasted the food? What if we adopted very firm opinions about our conclusions simply by reading the menu? That is how most people mistake their beliefs for actual reality.

By reading the menu, we create a concept of what we believe reality will be, but tasting the food is experiencing what the food actually is. We create an expectation in our imagination from reading the menu while we reference past experiences of what we liked and haven't liked. All that changes with the first bite.

We don't have to lie to ourselves about the food. We all know as soon as we taste it whether we like it or not. Do we have to believe or disbelieve anything the menu said once we have tasted the food for ourselves, or does our direct experience make the menu totally arbitrary? What if someone else tastes the same meal and has a different experience? Can you see that the perspectives are equally true for each person? What if they yuck your yum or love what you hate?

It is nearly impossible to maintain any kindness or humanity if we don't first realize this universal truth. Every person has a limited perspective that is purely unique. When we are mistaking our personal experience for the whole of possible experiences, even something as small as sharing our individual experience of a meal, the conclusions that we draw can lead to conflict.

I'll bet if I ordered a pepperoni pizza for a group of friends, most people would be fine with that. What if I told you that my favorite toppings are pepperoni and anchovies? What if I then further confessed that my favorites are actually pepperoni, anchovies, and pineapple? How do you react?

If food disagreements are too unimportant for you, think about politics, the news media, or religion. Can you see the same dynamic at work? Each person's limited perspective of beliefs is being compared to others' perspectives, and when they don't match we can become confused or upset, just like the prisoners.

It feels so satisfying when people affirm us and so frustrating or concerning when they disagree. We judge our perspective as "right" if we believe it, and "wrong" when we disbelieve. Exactly like with Nick and Santa.

That is the direct experience that shows us we are the prisoners in the cave, mistaking our limited perspectives for the whole of reality. If someone challenges the unrealized beliefs that we have mistaken for truth, we react negatively. The imposition of will begins, and we violate the Golden Rule by judging others or ourselves. That is when we fall into the duality of punishments and rewards.

> *The mind is not a vessel to be filled,*
> *but a fire to be kindled.*
> *—Plutarch*

To find what is truly going on within ourselves and out in the world, we have to be both curious and honest. Honest questions are the key to exploration. They are how we examine our legless chicken assumptions. I like to call them "quest-ions," because we will find what we are looking for. If the quest-ions come from negative emotions, like negatively charged ions they will lead only to bias confirmation and the threat response. Whenever we make that mistake—and we all have—it becomes instantly and absolutely vital to be "right," or we, like the prisoners in the cave mistaking their perceptions for reality, become confused or upset. If the quest-ions come from honesty and the curiosity of the true path, they will lead away from conflict and toward the wisdom of functionality and realization, as well as the perspective of the whole.

Ask yourself this quest-ion: Who creates or accepts beliefs?

Slow down, take a deep breath, and really think about it. Isn't it different from person to person? Isn't it subjective based on each person's individual perspective? If belief is created, denied, or accepted by each individual, how is that different from Truth?

Truth is not created by anyone, but applies to everyone equally. It is objective and based on observation of function and not personal conclusions. It is the perspective of the whole. Like how gravity functions. Regardless of what anyone believes about it, those beliefs have no impact on how it functions. A huge difference between the two is that belief is always a function of the limited, individual perspective. It is something that each person creates, accepts, or rejects, regardless of actual reality.

I know that words like truth and wisdom are very loaded words, but I am only using them in terms of function. To move concepts into function, we have to inquire into unexamined concepts and assumptions. Those are our legless chickens. We must ask our quest-ions. This is what I mean when I suggest making nouns into verbs. The noun is the fixed concept, and examining it in real-time experience is the functioning reality, regardless of expectation, definition, or hypothesis. Make sense?

> *The clues to solve any problem are in the patterns.*
> —*Steven Fidler*

Look around you. Look at the world. Look at nature. Better yet, close your eyes and go inside. Look at your body. This world, with all of its systems and seasons, functions effortlessly. Have you ever noticed that everything in life has a pattern? There are patterns, or cycles, in the days and the seasons. The cycles of life and death. These cyclical patterns are universal to us all.

Spring is birth, summer is the full flower of life, fall is the fading of that intensity into a richness of color and softer beauty, and winter finishes the cycle by allowing for rest. A time of pause before the cycle begins again.

There is a cycle in each day, as well. We have the birth of the day at sunrise, the spring of the day in the morning and early afternoon, the fall of the day into evening, and the darkness of night as the sun sets. Who or what designed this world in which all the seasons, the mountains and rivers, and the air that we breathe coalesce into what sustains all our lives, even as our bodies' trillions of cells support our life processes effortlessly? All of that, while mirroring back to us the cycles of death and rebirth in every day and the yearly cycle of the seasons!

. . .

Can you see the larger pattern that unifies all these things? When we are born, it is like the new birth of spring. Through our teens and twenties, we grow into the vibrant energy of summer. A bit later in life, that energy begins to ebb. Eventually we fall into the winter of old age and death. Then the cycle of rebirth begins all over again.

The same pattern is in the days. Each new day, born at dawn, grows into full vibrancy at noon, along with the temperatures of the day, then begins to fall off as afternoon fades into evening. Each day's death coming with the night. All of reality is made up of interwoven patterns. All the functions have a pattern. Including our behaviors. How, then, do so many things go so wrong in our lives and the world? It's because we mistake belief for reality.

What would happen if people believed that they "should" wear their summer clothes in winter, and their winter clothes in summer? Imagine people at the beach. The sun is shining, it's 85 degrees. The waves are rolling in and the smell of suntan lotion is in the air.

Now imagine that everyone at the beach is wearing multiple layers of clothing—heavy coats and those big, clunky winter boots. Imagine trying to play volleyball or surf in those outfits!

Now imagine the opposite. Picture everyone in their skimpy outfits, on the snow- and ice-covered beach in mid-winter. Surfing the freezing waves and playing volleyball in their bare feet in the snow and ice. That would be absurd, right? What if there was some old, unexamined law or some requirement that said this was the proper way to do things, regardless of personal experience or the degree to which the belief functioned? If we leave belief out of it and just look at function, would it be fair to say that the degree of functionality depends on how well we align with the reality of the underlying patterns?

If our beachgoers follow those beliefs and try harder and harder to make them work, will that make things better? Do they need to believe anything to make things work, or would everything work if they simply aligned with reality regardless of personal perspective?

Wouldn't it also be true that the degree to which they align with reality would correlate directly with how much better things would function? Imagine that first summer rule-breaker taking off one glove. They would notice the difference in their personal experience and might consider removing their jacket, regardless of the protestations of the believers, right?

Think of all the mental, physical, and emotional suffering caused by wearing all that heavy clothing at the beach in summer. Think of the increased chances for injury. Wouldn't it be the same for winter? It would literally affect every aspect of the experience—what we thought, said, and did.

Here is the fun part. Just like the patterns of the days, the seasons, and our lives, there are universal, self-evident patterns that apply to all of us without exception.

Could the suffering created by not aligning with the patterns of actual reality end by simply aligning fully with it? What if all our mental and emotional suffering is only the result of us being out of alignment with a reality that we don't have to create? What if all anyone has to do is align with the whole of how reality functions in order for everything to work?

THERE IS ONLY PRACTICE

If nouns are concepts, and verbing nouns are how the concepts actually function, then everything we do is the truth of who and how we are in any given moment. Everything we ever think, say, or do is our practice. When we think we are not practicing, that is a practice. Lying around on the couch is a practice. How and what we eat is a practice.

All practice forms patterns. Even now, the way we are is a full expression and reflection of every choice we have ever made in practice. Every thought we have ever had, every word we have ever spoken, and every action we have or haven't taken has resulted in us being exactly how we are in this very moment. Practice is how things function in real time. What does that mean? Remember when I was anxious and having panic attacks after losing my sight? I ate lots and exercised rarely. Those practices made me put on weight. I lay around a lot. My body began to pattern couch and not gym.

All the things I was afraid of while growing up, throughout grade school and high school as well as at home, formed patterns of worry. That, then, created neurology.

My fears of others finding out about my vision, my fears about public speaking, and on and on and on became patterns because it was my practice. That is what it means to feed the wrong wolf. I didn't know I was doing it, but by worrying about so many things I was forming habits, as well as neurology.

When I was in college, anger and judgment became my habits—how I abused myself and other people—because they were my practice. Can you see how, regardless of whether it's getting into or out of shape, developing a fear of public speaking, or becoming ass-holey as anyone can be, versus developing beneficial skills like being kind to ourselves and others, it is a practice that forms a pattern? The only difference is which wolf we are feeding and which neurology we are creating. Those are the two paths.

There are other practice patterns that feed the good wolf and create healthy neurology. Facing personal fears by encouraging yourself and others or learning to be patient and kind to yourself and other people, instead of judging yourself or them, builds trust and confidence and helps you to forgive. We are always learning to be skilled at being un-skilled, or skilled in ways that work. Everything is just patterns that we embody, resulting from what we practice and where.

There are lots of ways to see the truth in function. The more we look at function with genuine curiosity, the more truths we will recognize.

FUNCTIONAL TRUTH IS FOUND
IN THE PATTERNS OF EXPERIENCE

Here is another truth to find in your own experience: Whatever we focus on, we feed. When I focused on anxiety and tried to avoid that pain by distracting myself with food, it didn't relieve the anxiety. It gave me a temporary sense of relief from the pain, but the root problem was still waiting for me when the distraction ended.

That pattern of stress-eating only got reinforced by creating the re-peating cycle of anxiety triggering pain and panic, then food distracting from the pain. That is the process of addiction, and that is how anyone can get to over 300 pounds.

No one ever taught me anything other than practice makes perfect. After realizing the anxiety and stress-eating habit patterns that made me obese and kept me from leaving the house for five years, I realized the full truth of pattern creation. Habit patterns go in both directions. The reality is that practice can make both perfect and imperfect.

Think back to the story of the prisoners in Plato's cave. Plato is show-ing how the prisoners, by defining and labeling the shadows cast on the cave walls, mistake personal definitions and beliefs for reality. In the sto-ry of the three blind men and the elephant, the teacher is showing us the way each blind man mistakes his limited perspective for the whole of re-ality. In the story of the wise man in the village who doesn't create beliefs based on events, aren't we being shown the difference between a false reality created by the villagers when they draw conclusions about each event—again, depending on what they consider "good" and "bad"—and the whole of reality?

The parable of the three blind men and the elephant, the story of the wise man in the village, the Simone Biles story, my adventures with Nick and Bob, the stories of my childhood struggles with fear, and the stories about my anger in college—what are their patterns?

Which emotions fueled my "problems," and which solved them? What wolf was I feeding? What stories did I have to believe to maintain or change my patterns, and what patterns do these stories all have in common? Are you beginning to see the differences between the limited, selfish perspective and the perspective of the whole? Whether the stories come from our personal experiences or from the wisdom teachers, the function of the whole perspective or the dysfunction of mistaking our personal perspectives for reality is in the patterns.

In Plato's cave, when the prisoner's false realities were challenged they got upset and confused. When the three blind men began comparing their experiences of the elephant, they didn't realize they were comparing their limited perspectives. They were confused about how the others could be having a different experience, then became upset and started fighting. What emotions are involved every time we get upset? It's the negative ones. The path of the wrong wolf.

How can we break free of those bonds, venture out of our personal caves, and find that deeper reality? We must shift our perspectives from labeling, judging, and defining to curiosity and examining the moving parts of our experience in real time. We must learn to recognize the patterns. We have to move away from our limited personal definitions and look at how things function as a whole.

PATTERN RECOGNITION

One of the many ways we can tell the difference between truth and belief is that truth can be tested in real time for its self-evident functionality—right here, right now—and it is universal. Beliefs, if not testable, only have value to that individual believer and their limited perspective. It is the difference between reading the menu and imagining how the food tastes—and actually tasting the food.

Gravity works exactly the same for me as it does for you, right? So do anger and fear. When the fight-or-flight response is triggered, we all get dumber instantly because the blood rushes out of the area of the brain where good decisions are made and into the muscles preparing to fight or flee. This is universally true. We all share in the inability to realize when that threat response has been triggered, because we are instantly dumber. We then fall into cycles of guilt, shame, and blame, getting upset about how things should have been. How things should have been according to what? We fully mistake the limited self for reality and believe that thoughts plus feels equals reality.

A universal truth about all beliefs is that they can only come from the limited, selfish perspective. Personal beliefs are never universal. Even though large groups may believe in the same general idea, never does everyone believe in the exact same way. For example, according to Reference.com, there are nearly 41,000 denominations of Christianity. Which is the "right" one? Which are the "wrong" ones? It always goes back into personal debates from personal perspectives, trying to make the limited perspective the "truth" for the whole.

If, as the wisdom teachers say, we are all born thinking that our personal perspectives are the whole of reality, there must be certain qualities and characteristics of both paths. There must be patterns of functional truths that apply to everyone regardless of what we believe, patterns that we can all recognize so that we can learn the difference between our limited perspectives and the perspective of the whole. No one can give us the truth about the food on the menu by describing it for us. To see this for yourself, I will now do my best to move from telling you to showing you, but you will have to put yourself in my shoes. You will have to relate to my experiences.

We are all struggling with something in life, and we all have the same two neurological paths. We also all suffer from the exact same problem. It is self-evident in the pattern. We have mistaken our personal beliefs for reality, and when that is challenged, we become confused or upset.

For much of my life I had mistaken my limited personal point of view, and the negative emotions within it, for the whole of possible reality. I had no understanding that my personal perspective, and all personal perspectives, are made up of the same two parts: the stories we tell and the negative emotions that justify them. Taking back my journey and my full right to choose for myself has shown me the difference.

THE GIFT OF BLINDNESS

We think that life is happening to us, but truly it is happening for us. When our threat response is triggered, we fall into that limited, fearful, or angry perspective without realizing it. Then we inadvertently feed the negativity when we focus on it, reinforcing the cycle of dysfunction, creating a pattern. I fell deeply into this pattern of thinking when I lost my sight. The way I defined my blindness made me suffer even more. Fear and anxiety warped my perspective, and I spiraled down into cycles of distraction and destruction with food. The people around me labeled and defined my situation in a way that only supported the negative path.

I did graduate from college with honors, but despite my great grades, no one would hire me. I was offered a job, got the handshake that I thought confirmed the deal, and then got "unhired" over the weekend after I confessed that I was going blind. How was I going to survive, let alone live a meaningful life? It took about 10 years and never giving up to weather my storm.

During that time, while I was discarded by so many people that I thought were friends, as well as family and the job market, I was given one amazing gift: time. Lots and lots of time. It was only after my breakthrough on my journey that I discovered that all of life is a gift.

THE JOURNEY

At the beginning of my blindness, the emotional pain of the loss of my sight resulted from the sudden disconnection. I hadn't realized the extent to which everything that we ever do in life involves sight—that is, until that morning when I awoke to find that I would never see my Christmas lights again.

Sight is used for everything. We use it to see how we look in the mirror, how we decide to dress, what things get our attention when we are shopping, or when we see someone we find attractive. Even how we get from one end of a room to the other. Without exception, we look at our destination and keep looking at it until we get there. Since that December morning, all of that was replaced by a permanent disorientation.

Without sight, you never know anything for certain. You don't know where you are in space, who is or isn't in the room, how you look, or where you might want to go. Since I couldn't make eye contact, people stopped talking to me directly, instead talking about me with the people I happened to be with. It was incredibly isolating.

When I traveled, I would get questions like, "Where is your handler? Isn't there anyone helping you?" When I went to a restaurant on my own, which happened rarely, I would get the same questions. Life, directly lived or fully chosen, was the first thing to go.

In time, I found that I could adjust to the uncertainty of the disorientation, but the inability to easily interact with people and do things that I wanted to do was profoundly painful, both mentally and emotionally.

Where I once just decided I wanted to go and do something, now I had to engineer a way to do anything. Whether it was getting to the gym or making a sandwich, nothing was simple or efficient anymore.

All I could see in the beginning were the downsides. I was lost in the suffering of my anxiety and frustration about my new limitations. I was lost in the loss. I couldn't drive. I couldn't engage people with eye contact or see the expressions on their faces. Everything about fear told me to hide. I was stunned when I found out how much weight I had gained, and I was too afraid and depressed to face it. I didn't want anyone to see how far I had fallen, so I avoided everyone and tried to avoid facing the painful isolation of my reality by distracting myself with more food.

There came a time when I got so frustrated about being so fat and having no control over my panic and anxiety, as well as the depression from my isolation, that I wanted to die. That was when I went to the "right" wrong doctor.

HITTING THE BOTTOM

The only good thing about hitting rock bottom is
that the only way to go is up
—Anonymous

You may have heard about hitting rock bottom. I didn't know how far there was left to fall, but with all the extra weight and all the depression and anxiety, I woke up one morning to a perfectly round bald patch on the left side of my head, just above my ear.

It was about the size of a silver dollar pancake. I had no idea that literally overnight, high stress levels could result in a freakish, perfectly smooth circle, as if some miniature aliens had made a crop circle on my head while I was sleeping.

It was so bizarre! I couldn't even find the hair. It was just gone. This was the last straw. It was time for a serious change, so I set up an appointment with my doctor.

The day of the appointment, I showed up totally ready. I was ready to commit to whatever level of dedication and lifestyle changes would be required for me to end all this suffering and struggle.

The doctor came in, sat down, opened the folder he was carrying, and started reading. He just sat there, reading. That is, until he yawned. He stood up and went back to the door. He only said that I was a chubby boy and needed to accept the fact that I would be on anti-anxiety medication for the rest of my life, regardless of what I wanted. Then he walked out.

I was stunned. He had no interest in what I wanted out of life or the intensity of my suffering. He completely disregarded my frustration with my weight and panic attacks. That is when I realized that life is happening for us and not to us. By doing that, he pissed me off.

I hated how out of shape I was and the fact that I couldn't leave the house without my anxiety medication. I even had panic attacks about the medication when I dared to go out of the house and forgot to bring it. For me, the pills had become a reminder of how disempowered I felt from my ongoing struggles with anxiety. I wanted to find a way to solve it without medication.

By defining me and deciding the limitations of my life, that doctor motivated me to prove him wrong! With that decision, I had unknowingly created a new story that began a new pattern. A new reason to find my way through the cycle of anxiety and distraction with food. This doctor's attitude and disregard had gotten me in touch with pure rage. I was done waiting. I wasn't going to let anyone tell me what I couldn't do. Especially not this smug, condescending ass-hat.

Fueled by all the pain and frustration from years of fruitless struggle, I started exploring the fear. I went home, and each time I started to panic, I gritted my teeth and began looking at what was happening during the panic attack. To the best of my ability, with whatever clarity I could find, I calmed down and began watching my body react to whatever triggered the panic. I began to examine how it functioned. And I saw that it had a pattern.

Over time, as things continued to change, enough of the fight-or-flight response cleared and I began to see new possibilities in the self-defeating cycle of anxiety. My new mantra, "I will prove him wrong," began offering new possibilities with other things. Even with how I viewed my blindness.

Nothing that happens to us is ever purely good or bad.
Both of them are in there if we look.
—Meka

Since I was coming from a more empowered place, I began to realize new aspects of not seeing. I noticed that, without visual stimulus, there was less distraction. Without being able to look outward anymore, I found I could more easily look inward. I began examining the dynamics of the fear in myself.

I finally restored some sense of homeostasis to my nervous function and threw away the last of my anxiety medications. For years, I kept that empty prescription bottle as a trophy, to remind myself of what I had overcome.

Once I had some peace of mind restored, I began to look at my situation. How was I going to solve the seemingly impossible problem of having a life? Not the life that I had dreamed of before blindness, but just finding a way to make a living. How was I going to make a life out of this situation that I had defined as so limited, thanks to a ton of help from my family, my friends, and every system in society? I decided that I would, no matter what, find a way. I would never give up. That was the first key on my journey.

I had no idea about the two wolves or the two paths at that time, but by making that choice I unknowingly began to feed the good one, as well as creating neurology that supported it.

It took months for me to build some momentum in a better direction, but committing to that one simple thing made more things possible. I am not kidding when I tell you that one path is only possibilities, and the other is only limitation. Fear is paralytic that feeds the wrong-hearted wolf. Every doubt that we ever have engenders a hesitation that stops us from trusting. It stops us from moving forward. There literally can't be a journey with fear. Only more paralysis. Did you ever hear of analysis paralysis? Overthinking things to the point of complete indecision? That is what anxiety did for me.

After a few more years of struggling with obesity, anxiety, depression, and blindness, but fueled by the desire to find a way out, I heard an advertisement for massage school as a career option and, like a switch, a light went on inside of my mind.

After I lost my sight, no one had seen any value or use for me. But I believed in myself, so I decided that I was going to start my own business. That is what led me to contact services for the blind in the state of Washington.

My experiences with government services have varied greatly from state to state. Depending on the perspective of the person who is administering those services, it can be either humiliating or empowering. Again, the two paths. Who knew that going to massage school would be the breakthrough that changed my life? When I made a commitment to showing up and trying new things, possibilities started to appear. They culminated in the synchronicity of two seemingly unrelated events.

THE TURNING POINT

I had just watched the documentary *The Secret* when I met with my case worker, Vicky Lyons. I had already started massage school, but I got inspired after watching that movie. Another event that happened was totally uninspiring as well.

Massage school was going fine until there was a single class on something they had called "abreactions." An abreaction is a strong, unexplainable emotional response that a client experiences during massage. The only tool they gave was to just be with that person, letting them know they aren't alone and that things will be all right. Basically, to just ride it out with them. Good advice in practice but, being blind, I was very uncomfortable with this as my only tool. I wouldn't be able to see the look on the client's face. I wouldn't be able to see what they might try to do or what they might need. So much could go wrong.

Because of that class, I contacted Vicky. I wanted to change the plan that she had already approved and funded, but it was too late for any changes. I set up another appointment anyway, and she visited me again. I voiced my concerns to her and explained that I had come up with an idea. I could develop a secondary tool that would both help people if this abreaction scenario ever arose and expand what I could offer in my business: I could also certify in hypnotherapy.

I had no idea what it was at the time, but Vicky authorized every part of the expanded plan. It turned out that she had just watched *The Secret* as well, and she, too, was inspired by it. My own inspiration from watching it, as well as the passion I had for my potential, created a feeling of momentum between us during that conversation.

We bonded over that movie and we both felt inspired. It was a great meeting, and she left after chuckling about how she was going to expand my plan as her final action before her retirement. That wasn't the only synergy of synchronicity that was going to happen. Unknowingly, I was building momentum toward truly changing my life forever. All change starts somewhere, and, for me, it began with massage school.

Going to massage school was quite the challenge for me. I hadn't been out of the house for years, and although I had gotten better at managing my panic and anxiety, I had a long list of new fears that I hadn't had when I was sighted. Remember, I had the idea that I was worthless while growing up, from that diaper incident as well as other things.

After I became blind, I found myself worrying about being judged by people because I no longer had any idea what I looked like. I was still a heavily muscled guy, but I had been through gaining over 300 pounds and truly believed that I was fat and ugly. I worried that I would be judged harshly by the other massage students; many others, including friends, had left, so I had little support to navigate blindness. I had terrible body issues, and I had picked the one profession that required me to be the most vulnerable.

I was so much more than uncomfortable at the beginning of this new adventure. I can't list all the complexities involved, but it was quite the transition to go from years of being too afraid of having a panic attack to leave the house to waking up every morning at 5:00 a.m., getting on the bus at 6:00, and getting dropped off about five or six blocks from the school during the morning commuter rush in downtown Seattle. I had to learn to navigate all the people on the sidewalks, the noise and distractions, and the traffic crossings, relying on listening and tapping with a cane. All this just to arrive at school and have the opportunity to get naked and be massaged by strangers. Not stressful at all.

I remember many times when I easily could have died just from the commute. The school was downtown, at the bottom of a steep hill just off a main street. Until I lost my sight I had no idea how blind people know when to cross the street, but I learned that it is by listening for traffic in both directions and just guessing when it is safe to cross.

Seattle is a very environmentally conscious city and there are lots of electric cars. Battery-powered cars are silent, so there was nothing to hear. I can't tell you how many times I was midway across the street and realized an electric car was approaching, and I had to pray that the driver would stop in time. Most other vehicles, including large buses, would just turn onto the steep road that I had to cross every day and coast silently down the hill.

Throw that on top of the body issues, being massaged by strangers, the schoolwork, and bussing to the gym after class and getting home each day around 7:00 at night. It was exhausting, both mentally and physically.

I went to school four days a week for nine months, but during that time I rediscovered that I had an advantage: my own determination. Despite my struggles with panic, anxiety, and depression, I had made a commitment to myself. Even though no one saw any future for me or offered much support, the fact that I was determined to find a way no matter what gave me strength.

I challenged the fear that I had fed during my struggle with panic and anxiety. I stopped hiding and began to feed my possibilities. Even in the class in which we learned about abreactions, I didn't hide from my discomfort. I didn't quit school or decide not to practice massage. I found a way forward. I decided to get more tools. I began to realize that just being on the good path creates more and more possibilities.

For the first time, I was using my fear and anger instead of them using me. Fear wasn't stopping me anymore, and that built my courage and confidence. I wasn't using anger to hurt myself or anyone else, because I was using it as fuel to prove that doctor and everyone else wrong! I told myself that if I did get hit by a car or a bus, I would make one hell of a dent in that car or bus before it took me down. I was using all that anger to build momentum.

I wasn't dwelling on my limitations; I had committed to finding a way. I didn't like who or how I was, but the pain of my situation gave me the strength to challenge my circumstances. I still had to find a hypnotherapy program, but despite that and the possibilities created by the effort and pain I was facing, my determination to forge ahead changed everything.

FINDING MY WAY

I wasn't from the Seattle area, but I knew some people who went to the naturopathic medical school nearby. It's considered the best alternative medical school in the country, so I thought that someone there might be able to recommend a good teacher.

To my surprise, all the people who responded recommended the same person: Jack Elias.

I looked him up and read about what he offered. I was interested immediately because he was a lifelong practitioner of Buddhism and had synthesized Buddhist practice with hypnotherapy. I had zero experience with or knowledge of Buddhism and no understanding of hypnotherapy, but I was still searching for a spiritual connection after my semi-failed attempt in college.

My experience with hypnotherapy was the beginning of a depth of understanding, because it revealed the functions of the mind. Not what people believed or what I believed, but how things actually work for all minds. I am fortunate to have had a true teacher in Jack. He realized and conveyed dynamics in such a way that I could feel the depth in the implications. I began contemplating and applying what I had learned from him, and after 13 years, I am writing this book.

Without Jack and Vicky, I would not be who I am today. Without facing all the fears of the commute and the issues that came up day to day in class, I would not have completed massage school or found hypnotherapy. Without blindness I would not have gone down this road, and without what I learned after Vicky retired, none of this journey could have happened in the first place. This is what I mean when I say that life is not happening to us, it is happening for us.

Personal growth doesn't come cheap. It always comes through struggle. It's like the growing pains that we feel while growing up, but personal growth hurts because we are challenging our limiting beliefs and negative emotions. All growth is uncomfortable, because it always involves facing our fears, forgiving the hurts of anger, or learning to be kind to our sadness. Whether it comes by facing our fear of giving a speech in front of people, changing jobs, or losing a relationship, what we first identify as pain is always an opportunity for growth, if we just commit to following it to its end and trusting the growth process.

After Vicky retired, I learned from the person who replaced her that the state only allows for one training. One single program. I should not have been allowed any funding except for massage school.

Vicky had approved at least three trainings that I can remember. I was inspired by the possibilities of these extra trainings, as well as my vision for how to use them. She had funded my entire vision for my path. She banked on humanity and not on the definitions and limits of the system. Whether overfunding my training was a mistake or intentional, my approach was authentic. That authenticity is what brought the rest of what I discovered and what I am sharing with you now.

By allowing myself to try to find a future, I had unconsciously shifted away from accepting all the negative definitions that were limiting me around my blindness, as well as the limitations of my family, society, and my potential. With that shift in perspective, I had moved out of negativity into possibility. I had challenged my limiting beliefs and gotten a glimpse of the wholeness of function.

At the time, I didn't realize the full implications of what I am writing now, but during the hypnotherapy training I did sense something. A deeper realization than I had experienced before. Curiosity and genuine inspiration overrode the negativity, and as I practiced hypnosis as my teacher's unique approach to de-hypnosis, I began to see the patterns of the two paths. The key was in my direct experiences while working with Jack and my class during the training.

If all those wisdom teachings that I mentioned before—Plato's allegory of the cave, the parable of the three blind men and the elephant, and the wise man in the village—are correct, and we are all missing the mark by mistaking our limited perspectives for reality, the beginning of my realization of this began on day one of my hypnotherapy training.

THE POWER OF DIRECT EXPERIENCE IN CONTEXT

We started with a simple exercise. We were supposed to relax and let something bubble up from the past. There were nine of us in the class, and we split off into practice groups to do our first regression practice sessions.

Regression just means visiting something from the past, so we were going to relax and let some limiting belief come up. It was the first time doing hypnotherapy for all of us, and everyone had a bit of nervous, curious energy. In my practice group, I was the first subject and I got to work with a psychiatrist and another person who had a master's degree in psychology.

Wouldn't you know it, but the very first thing that came up for me was the diaper incident from my childhood! As I shared the memory, I heard something that no one wants to hear from a trained therapist: both the psychiatrist and the psychologist gasped. Until that moment, I'd thought that my story wasn't that bad, but to hear two highly trained professionals gasp at the story, given everything they had heard during their long careers, a voice in my head said, "Shit. Maybe I am more damaged than I thought." That is when Jack gently stepped in.

He took in the whole scene. He saw that the two trained and experienced professionals were stunned and, being new to hypnotherapy, were at a loss as to how to proceed. He realized exactly what was going on and provided all of us with a lesson in function.

The beautiful thing about regression therapy is that a memory comes up as if you are watching a video of it in your mind's eye. Hypnotherapy is all about overcoming limiting beliefs that hold us back, and this was one of my deepest misunderstandings. I had equated myself with the family dog; I had a general sense of being less than others.

Jack took me right up to the point of the trauma in the memory and told me to pause the scene. This is where the magic started. We played with the memory. At this point, instead of reliving the trauma, he encouraged me to bring my current self into the scene. I lifted that little version of me up, kindly put him on my shoulders, and handed him the poopy diaper, which he joyfully shoved in my mom's and my brother's faces.

I nearly began to laugh out loud. In the first 15 minutes, in my very first hypnotherapy experience, Jack had guided and encouraged me through one of the biggest traumas of my life—and it was transformed into a new possibility. My limiting belief was no longer a fixed, uncontested "reality." That was the moment when I began to unravel my Matrix. I saw that ALL belief is self-hypnosis. After that, I began to learn the difference between belief and the functional reality of direct experience.

To begin to take back our journey, we must reconnect to our true hearts and true minds. The genuine us is always still there, underneath all that conditioning and definition. Underneath all those paintings of who we think we are and how we have to be to be acceptable to ourselves and others. The truth of all of life is waiting behind the limitation of what we believe.

Since we have all been defining ourselves and the shadows cast on the walls of the caves in our minds, we have to begin to see the signs and symptoms of the Matrix running in the background of our limited perspectives.

If you take nothing else from reading this book, take this next statement to heart. *The quality of our lives is completely determined by which emotions we feel and choose to focus on, as well as the stories that we tell. We get to choose those things. It is the combination of those two things that make up our beliefs.*

I didn't realize before I took the hypnotherapy training with Jack that my past traumas weren't permanent and impossible to heal. I thought the conclusions I had drawn, and the way I had been treated, were carved in stone. A permanent historical record of who I was and how the world is. I had no idea that I was thinking the thoughts, that I was drawing the conclusions, and that my negative emotions were causing the pain that I didn't know how to heal. So I projected the stories and reasons that I had come up with onto myself and the world. They were the shadows on the walls of my allegorical cave, me mistaking my self-limiting perspective for the whole of reality, and my conclusions about the events in the village as to what was "good" and "bad."

That regression session was the beginning of my shift. The pain of the diaper incident was one of the earliest and deepest pains that I had. Playing with the scene, as well as the story and the outcome, changed my emotions, which then began to change my neurology. I had been tricked into believing that the conclusions I drew in the past were the fixed reality of the future; that upsetting thoughts plus feelings equals reality, instead of realizing that I had mistaken the limiting beliefs in my personal perspective for what was possible.

My direct experiences showed me that I had forgotten something after I created the beliefs—that I was the one naming the shadows. Then, I remembered the most powerful thing. Regardless of which path of belief I was feeding—fear or love—it is I who gets to choose.

TAKING BACK THE JOURNEY: OUR FREE-WILL CHOICE

How can we begin to see the shadows on the walls of Plato's cave within us? How can we take back our journey, restore our ability to respond appropriately? We have to get involved with our journey instead of defining it. We need to learn that every limiting definition that anyone has ever imposed on us that makes us "responsible" to something or someone, including ourselves, is coming from the limited selfish perspective with its rewards and punishments. The fear of loss and the desire to gain.

> *Which of you by taking thought can*
> *add one cubit unto his stature?*
> *—Jesus of Nazareth, from the Book of Matthew 6:27*

We have all been taught that thinking is prime. No one ever told us that thinking can mean imagining things hypothetically. Due to a lifetime of labeling, judging, concluding, and assuming, we have mistaken thinking for the reality of direct experience. All thinking is words, and all words are just made-up labels to communicate some idea. The idea that thoughts are things. The idea of a table, a person, your friend, or your enemy. It's taking a real-time, ever-changing reality and freezing it in time. Making the waterfall into a video of a waterfall. No matter how much you might insist that that is a real waterfall, your hand will never get wet when you touch the picture.

Here is how useful thinking is: I challenge you to spend the 10,000 hours it takes to master anything just by thinking. Read every book you can. Read all the data, gather all the facts. If it is about music and you want to play an instrument or sing, go and "learn." Read, conceptualize, think, and think more about it. If it's about martial arts, fighting strategy, execution of technique, and so on, read and think about it.

If you now believe you know all about a topic—martial arts, for example—go spar with a martial artist who has been practicing for 10,000 hours. Go do a concert with a musician or singer who has been playing or singing for 10,000 hours. Then you will begin to see the difference between thinking and the real-time function of wisdom. What we believe we know, as opposed to what we can actually live.

For most of my life, I made that same mistake. While I was growing up, I was told what and who to believe. Who was good and what was bad. I did what everybody does. When I got old enough, I challenged what I was taught.

I went to religion and when that didn't work, I went to self-help. When I was reading self-help and thinking about helping myself, I was never actually living the part that helps. It was the same with my beliefs about God in college. When all spiritual teachings share the same foundational emotions of Love, Peace, and Joy and the same teachings of function, it was never a problem with the teachings. I was mistaking thinking about them, and drawing conclusions, for living them.

I had to stop trying to prove to myself and everyone else that my beliefs were "right" and start facing my fears and forgiving my anger. I never lived the good parts. I just understood the concepts and redefined them to try to force reality to conform to my limited perspective. I named the shadows on my cave wall and called the ones I liked "good" and the ones I didn't like "evil," and I thought that gave me the right to judge others and punish or reward them based on the degree to which they affirmed or denied my limited perspective. The certainty that I invested in my conclusions gave me a sense of knowing something. But isn't actual knowing the degree to which you can embody it right now, in the present time?

BE KIND TO YOURSELF

I remember the day Jack asked me to examine the reality of how I was treating myself. I remember him asking this powerful question: "Can you tell yourself that you love yourself and mean it with your whole heart and soul?"

As soon as I asked myself the question, I was instantly uncomfortable. It felt so awkward when I thought about it. I was like "Yep, done, Jack." I nodded my head yes and mumbled a dismissive "uh huh" to let him know that I was finished with this exercise, but he didn't move on.

He slowed me down and asked, "Can you say it out loud?" I couldn't, so I paused. He asked me another question. "Do you love yourself?" I did what years of conditional love taught me to do. I lied.

I gave a weak "yes" in reply, hoping that he would just drop it and move on. Jack is a real teacher, though. He truly understands what I have come to call the two paths and has lived it for many more years than I have. So he called my bluff and made me move from concept to direct experience by saying this: "Do you really love yourself? If you do, there would be no fear or reason not to say it out loud, right? The words, 'I love you, Steve.'" It sounds so simple when you just think about it. It was much harder, though, to mean it.

I reluctantly said, "I love you, Steve," and in that moment, in my mind, I heard it. My mind screamed, "Of course I love me when I am not being such a fucking idiot and messing everything up! Of course I could, if I weren't such a blind loser without a job and a life!" The self-criticisms went on for a while, but that was the first time I fully realized how horribly I was treating myself.

I believed that I loved myself. I believed that I knew it for certain, but my reaction and the lengthy tirade of self-abuse in my mind at that moment showed me the truth. I had no idea of the difference between beliefs and reality. Limiting beliefs are just stories fused with negative emotions.

One of the things that happens when we mistake belief for reality is that we mistake the movement of our thoughts and emotions and our belief and meaning-creation for actual experience. It was exactly what fooled me into believing that I loved myself when I was just telling myself that to excuse the ways I abused myself. Again, Jack and that hypnotherapy course didn't just tell us about the concepts, we experienced them in real-time function.

Experience this for yourself. I am about to ask you to do what Jack had me do, so that you can start to see for yourself. When I ask you if you love yourself, what is your answer? Don't think about it, DO it and see what comes up, without judging it, to the best of your ability.

Now, say "I love you" and say your name out loud. Say it over and over and see how much you can mean it. Go now and do this in front of a mirror. Look yourself in the eye when you do it. See how much you can mean it with your whole heart and soul.

What is your experience like? Does it feel awkward or like a lie in some way? Can you openly proclaim it while smiling at yourself? Where in your body do you feel any resistance or joy? Do you feel your heart wide open, or do you feel the split where you love some parts, but not others? Do you feel something in you holding back?

The extent to which we can embody love for ourselves is a reflection of reality, and not what we say we believe. A mirror of how conditionally we love ourselves.

Did any reasons come up when you did it? Did you find that your negative thoughts tried to justify or rationalize the abuses? When I did it, the realization was amazing for me. I was completely unaware that I was treating myself so terribly, accepting the rationalizations and justifications coming from thoughts generated by negativity, as though I deserved the abuse.

If you think that was easy, let me offer up the advanced version. Go and tell yourself that you love yourself out loud, standing naked in front of a full-length mirror, while looking yourself in the eye. Keep repeating it while looking at each part of your body and see how much you can mean it. Can you begin to see the difference between the concept of loving yourself and the reality of it when you try to live it in the present time?

It amazed me how conditional my love for myself and other people was. How many times I had mistaken love for abuse by simply accepting whatever excuses were offered up by those negative emotions? I didn't realize how being negative disconnected me from my true heart, and my thinking and rationalizations disconnected me from my true mind.

THE ANSWER TO EVERY PROBLEM
IS IN THE PATTERN

Let yourself be silently drawn by the strange pull of
what you really love. It will not lead you astray.
—Rumi

If the answer is truly found in the patterns, then pattern recognition is a skill worth developing. What is the pattern of every problem? What happens each time something goes wrong in your, my, or anyone else's day? We get upset, right?

That is the signal. That is our chance. It is the transition point at which the unrealized negativity in the reaction makes us instantly dumber and moves us into our limited perspectives, combining the pain of negative emotions with the stories that they generate to justify the fight-or-flight reaction. To justify the excuses and abuses.

That is exactly what happened to me with the conclusions I drew from the diaper incident as a child. It happened again with Nick and Santa, Bob and public speaking. It was the same false reality that caused me to avoid the prom, to mistreat and judge everyone in college, and to be horrible to myself while telling myself that the abuse was deserved and that I was being loving and kind.

For many years, I was inadvertently feeding the wrong wolf by focusing on the negative emotions. I forgot all about the other neurological path. Rest, digest, and recover. How does one live that? If fight or flight is the two-sided coin of fear and anger, how can we activate the other path? We have to calm the F*** down and relax. You know I mean calm the FEAR down, right? It's not only about calming down. What we need to do is find a balance between the sympathetic and the parasympathetic, so that we can take the true-hearted path. I didn't realize that too much sympathetic will burn you out from pushing your way through life, while too much parasympathetic creates lethargy. Creating new patterns takes a bit of time, but as neuroplasticity has taught us, practice makes perfect…and imperfect. It is literally just a matter of taking the time to create either in our neurology.

At first, it was way easier to see into other people than it was to see inside myself. Once I saw the pattern so clearly in other people, I began to see it in myself. That pattern of getting confused or upset when some belief from the limited, personal perspective was challenged. They reacted negatively, each time becoming confused or upset.

The excuses for abuses that those emotions provided are easy to see in others when they get upset. It's not hard to see them get up to 30 IQ points dumber. We just have a harder time believing that we are no different when we get upset.

We aren't 30 IQ points dumber. When we get upset, it's perfectly justified. Those worries are important! Those punishments are all deserved. We totally forget our kindness and love. It's so easy to justify the reasons because of the negative emotions that we feel. It was only by looking at my excuses for how I abused myself and other people, while calling it love, that I was able to see reality. I realized that I had to become the change I wanted to see in the world, not just judge people or make up beliefs about them.

I made a commitment to live this and not just think about it, and the change began to come. By making that new commitment and acting instead of thinking, I was disrupting my old patterns and forming new ones.

THE PROCESS

The first thing I noticed was that I could not catch my upset reactions in the present time. The negative emotions were too overwhelming. I could only examine them later when I had calmed the f*** down. Then, I was able to recognize the negative emotions behind my reactions, and I could be kind and encouraging toward myself. I was able to forgive myself fully, asking others to forgive me when I had been negative toward them. These changes were the beginnings of interrupting and breaking down the old patterns.

The second step was adopting a new pattern. Simply training my mind to observe my reactions was, in and of itself, a new pattern, but more than that, I began a practice that lowered my reactivity and activated the path of relaxation. But nothing truly changed until I started to treat myself with kindness.

Every morning and every night, I began listening to guided meditations. In time, that practice lowered my baseline reactivity and replaced it with a centered calm. Then, the best thing happened. I began to support and encourage myself, instead of all that self-abuse, and I began to catch my reactions in real time.

Instead of being washed away by them, I saw them. Just as I did when I tried to tell me that I loved myself, I began to see my mind making up excuses for abuses. I began to breathe into the areas that I felt the tension, to train my nervous system to calm down and remain clear.

According to neuroscientist Dr. Jill Bolte Taylor, we have what I will call a golden window. From the moment we get upset, we have about one minute before we shift completely into our negative neurology and begin patterning it. During that minute, we can change things if we use our upset reactions as a signal to calm down, instead of a justification for making bad choices. Remember when we began this journey together and I said that we have a twofold lie of the heart and mind? That means our thoughts and emotions. We must calm down and let go of thinking to be here in the present moment. No thinking, just real time, moment by moment, directly experiencing and learning.

To restore the heart, we must realize that negative emotions can't have positive outcomes—but every negative emotion has a positive intention that it cannot fulfill.

The negative reactivity in every moment of upset keeps us focusing on and feeding what we don't want. We don't want to feel the pain in the loss or the pain in the want. All our negative emotions are signals of needing something, but what? What does fear want in order to solve the pain of worry and stress? Courage and encouragement. A feeling of safety and calm. It wants to know that it is okay to be afraid. Kindness and encouragement toward ourselves gives fear courage and lets us feel the emotion without fighting to control or avoid it.

What does anger want? It wants to be heard. We must acknowledge the pain of disempowerment if we hope for reconciliation. Anger represents the frustration of past events being unfulfilled, searching for a chance to reconcile—again, as in the dream about my brother and me. A chance to forgive ourselves and others and reconnect with our true hearts. These patterns are universal to us all. What does sadness want other than kindness and love to end the feelings of despair and loneliness?

Doesn't fear tell us to hide? Doesn't it tell us that we can only be safe if we run away from whatever threatens us? How can this solve fear? Wouldn't running away create a pattern that only feeds it? Anger says to punish people so they feel the pain that we feel, right? How can that lead to forgiveness? Sadness needs kindness to resolve itself, but all it ever did for me was try to protect me from the pain of losing relationships and people who were kind to me. I did this by ending those relationships or distancing myself from everyone, because I was sure that someday they would find out I wasn't worth being around and leave. Will following any of these emotions and their stories ever get us anywhere? Wouldn't it be better to calm the F*** down, remember what we truly want in our heart of hearts, and refocus on that?

A PATH WORTH COMMITTING TO

Until I realized this, the limiting beliefs that I created held the negativity that caused the pain I desperately wanted to end. I now realize that our reactivity is our opportunity. It gives everyone a chance to change. That neurology was built over time by practice and patterning. There is no science that says neurology isn't created in both directions. Remember, practice makes perfect *and* imperfect.

What would happen if we calmed the fear down and made that our new base level of reactivity? No one will ever worry their way to peace or punish their way to forgiveness. Once we see the pain in our negative emotions as a signal, we can realize what each negative emotion wants and go straight to it. Forgiveness through reconciliation is the antidote to anger. Not more punishments.

If we make these realizations our new pattern, would it even be possible for us to get triggered if we realized that all the judgments inside of ourselves and from others are just coming from limited perspectives? That all of it is our personal preferences, not the truth of who we are and how things should be?

If you were to remember that one single thing in every conversation you had with someone else, that would change your life completely! If you remembered, every time you talked to anyone, that both of you were coming from your personal limited perspectives whenever you gave opinions, judged anything or anyone, or created or adopted any belief, how could you ever take anything personally again? Better yet, how helpful could you be if you recognized that when people are upset, they are lost in their limiting fears and emotions? You can empathize with them rather than debating or evaluating their beliefs and conclusions.

Everyone has a right to their own perspective. They are all equally important. They are the beliefs of that person. They are not your truth, and your beliefs aren't the truth for anyone else. Could you take to heart anything negative that anyone said about you if you fully realized that they were talking about stories they have experienced from their personal perspective, generated by their personal emotions and their limited view of the world?

If we can own that, then we can know with absolute certainty that our journey is ours alone. Only we can define our journey. Only we can accept or create the beliefs that we use to navigate our way in the world. We can realize that only we can take things personally.

Our pain is our gift. When we become confused or upset, it is an opportunity to learn. To use the emotional pain instead of it using us. When we get upset, we can use it as a signal to interrupt the old pattern and form a new one.

If you want to take back your response ability, take back your choice in the moment. Calm down, get that 30 IQ points back, fill your heart with forgiveness, be kind to yourself, and make that a pattern. Make an absolute commitment to living that life and not thinking about it. Imagine what living from your true heart and soul would be like in 10 years if you started today. That is a life worth living and a heart worth giving.

The function or dysfunction of everything can be found in the pattern. You have the imposition of will to give you an instantaneous measure, in all situations, of who is mistaking their personal limited perspective for reality—and it becomes easier in time to recognize which emotions are driving everything. We can all be free of our mental and emotional suffering! Better yet, we can feed our true hearts and live with passion and purpose! With kindness and love!

The One Problem in the World
and the One Solution

There is nothing new under the sun.
—King Solomon, Ecclesiastes 1:9

WHAT WOULD THE WORLD LOOK LIKE if everyone mistook their personal limited perspective for the whole of the truth? Would people understand that they are part of the greater whole of humanity, and therefore honor themselves and all people equally? Or would they try to impose their will on others based on their own "truth," which is really just their desire for gain and fear of loss? Would everyone realize that we didn't create this world, but we do share it?

We've all heard the statement that the whole is made up of the sum of its parts. What if we could use the patterns we have discovered to fully and simply understand the function and dysfunction in our personal lives and in all the systems? Once we recognize the patterns in these two paths, all things quickly and easily make sense.

Personally honoring the Golden Rule by coming from the true-hearted emotions of love, kindness, and humanity, and not imposing our will on ourselves or others, is the path that actually functions, and no one's limited personal perspective can possibly function as the truth for the whole. These are the paths of the function and dysfunction of all things.

WE'RE ALL IN THE SAME BOAT

The two paths are not just in you and me. All the world's systems are made up of people, and we are all subject to the same two paths. But what if we have all been taught the same mistake? What if we were born into a system that has imposed its will on us without our knowledge or choice? What if, from the very moment we came into this world, we were taught that the limited perspective of another person or group of people must somehow be made to be the truth for all people? Could these very man-made systems, full of unexamined assumptions and beliefs, be the problem that can never be solved?

We would be like fish who were born into toxic water and don't recognize the toxicity of the water they are immersed in because they have never known anything else. If we are born into dysfunction and try to solve our problems from the level that only creates more dysfunction, is it surprising that things are as they are in the world around us?

There were problems in the world before we got here. We were born into them and taught what they mean by others. Those who taught us were born into the same misunderstanding, accepting the limited perspectives that they were taught instead of finding the truth of functional wisdom. Their parents, teachers, and societies did the same, and their predecessors did the same, on and on back to the beginning of all our histories. We have all mistaken the shadows on the walls of our personal caves for reality.

What if no one can find the solutions because no one is examining the root assumption that this is how things are and always will be? What if that failure to examine has perpetuated all the dysfunction and abuse in all the histories that we read about? A root legless chicken that we only need to examine in terms of function and dysfunction to see how our systems work and why they fail? What if all the wars, the atrocities, the greed, and the inhumanity that is happening, and has ever happened, have the same patterns that we can easily identify? If we can learn to recognize these patterns, we can change them. We can get free of dysfunction and create systems that function.

There are lots and lots of legless chickens inside of us that we are totally unaware of. Lots of assumptions about how things are and how they should be. There is also something in all of us that longs to be free from the pain and destruction and conflict in ourselves and the world.

How can one person's or one group's beliefs become rules that work for all people? Who can possibly know what you want and need out of life to find deep meaning and purpose, other than you? If it is true that no solution can come from the level of the problem, and the universal problem is mistaking the limited perspective for the whole truth, and that same problem is in all the people who create and define our systems of laws, government, and businesses, we will have to look to the level where solutions come from. The perspective of the whole.

It is my hope that you are beginning to see these two paths more clearly in yourself and the world around us. We all have sympathetic and parasympathetic nervous pathways. We all have our limited perspectives based in the fear of loss and the desire for gain. But all of us want to connect deeply and honestly to our lives and the experiences that we share with those we love. There is a part of us that holds our true desires. A part that is longing to be free from our emotional and mental pain and suffering.

> *Art imitates life.*
> —*Aristotle*

> *Life imitates art.*
> —*Oscar Wilde*

Once you start recognizing the two paths in all things, everything that seemed so difficult becomes simple. To see both paths more clearly, it really does help to look at our culture. They aren't just in our governments, businesses, and religious institutions; these dynamics exist in everything. Our movies, art, music, books, games, and poetry. The arts give us a way of experiencing something more than just words. A closer reflection of actual experience. Movies and music that move us, inspire us, or make us sad are mirrors for us to better see ourselves and others. Exploring a few different art forms can really help to identify the two paths in real time.

REPLACING TRUTH WITH BELIEF: THE IMPOSITION OF WILL

I am a big movie and music fan. I am not so much of a fan of the visual arts these days. Yeah, I've got jokes. One of my recent favorite movies is *Schindler's List*. It came out in 1994, and I saw it a few years after it was released. It is the true story of a German industrialist and entrepreneur who was credited with saving 1,200 Jewish workers from the forced labor camps during World War II. The story is powerful, not only because of the personal risk Schindler took to save people, but also because it is a perfect expression of both paths, as you will see.

The true path honors reality and all individual perspectives equally by honoring the Golden Rule, while the path of the limited, fearful self violates it through the imposition of will and always justifies it by a group's or individual's personal fears of loss and desires for gain. It is important to recap this because we are about to see the function and dysfunction of each of these paths through all our man-made systems.

In the movie *Schindler's List*, Oscar Schindler begins his journey as a failure in business. His father was a successful businessman, but Oscar has failed at every venture he has attempted. He knows how to navigate high society, though. He knows how to bribe and entertain officials. He is familiar with the game that the high-ranking and wealthy officers play. He also knows that the self-important want to believe their crimes aren't criminal. He is no different.

After all, Schindler is a member of the ruling Nazi party, and the Nazis are forcing people to work in labor camps under the direction of various so-called entrepreneurs or industrialists. We call them business-men today.

In the beginning of his new venture, Schindler is super excited. He has free labor, he is funded by the very people he is oppressing, and he can't lose. His company is making essential gear for the German military and the ongoing war effort, so his success is guaranteed.

Mr. Schindler, however, is a terrible businessman. He is not a de-tail-oriented guy. He needs someone who will keep track of all the books and paperwork and bribes, so he enlists Isaac Stern, one of the thousands of Jews forced into labor.

Mr. Stern doesn't share the giddy excitement of Schindler, however, as he watches his people get brutalized, tortured, and murdered. The only goal for him and all his people is survival. Schindler can't lose and Stern and his people can only hope to survive. It's not entirely different from the dynamics of global economic inequality today.

Schindler is excited about his situation because he is getting every-thing he wants. He is satisfying the hell out of his desire for personal gain, with absolutely no fear of loss.

Finally, after all his failures, he will prove to himself and others that he is not only as good as his father, but maybe even better. His goal is to leave the war with at least two gigantic chests full of money. Stern, on the other hand, is hoping to find a way to keep himself and his people safe and alive.

Since Schindler is pretty much just letting the money roll in while schmoozing with political officials and high-ranking military officers, Stern is left to run the business, which he does expertly.

In a short time, Schindler has enough money, even after paying all the requisite bribes and kickbacks, that he is riding high. Meanwhile, Stern takes advantage of the fact that Schindler isn't paying attention. He secretly uses the company as a refuge for those who are at highest risk of being put on the kill lists.

In time, Stern realizes that Schindler doesn't hate or abuse the Jewish workers in his company. He begins to build trust with Schindler, which slowly evolves into a friendship. That bond will change everything.

At this point in the story, Oscar is happy because he is making money like crazy. He has sent his wife away so that he can enjoy as many mistresses as he chooses, and he doesn't have to do anything because Stern is doing all the work. He has absolute power without taking any responsibility for the suffering of the people he is using for his personal gain. Is he any different from the wealthy and powerful today?

The very thought of anyone saying no to Schindler never enters his mind. What would happen if one of the workers said no? They would be executed on the spot. At this point, can you see the dynamic of every abusive situation on the wrong-hearted path? Were the Jews freely choosing to work, or were they coerced to work to serve another's will imposed on them?

In the context of the desire for personal gain and the avoidance of loss, there is no actual power over others. There is only the threat of consequences or a promise of rewards. The soldiers are rewarded for committing abuses and the enslaved are punished if they do not comply with the soldiers' demands. Oh, and if a member of the military doesn't commit the atrocities required of him? He is punished for not serving the will of the party. Are you beginning to see that these patterns are exactly the same today? The punishments and rewards are different, but the catering to the individual selfish perspective at the expense of everyone else is identical.

Schindler is in total denial about what is going on in the labor camps. He ignores the war completely, just as he ignores the suffering of the people he is using for his personal profit. His personal limited perspective is getting him everything that he has defined to consider himself a "success," and therefore he is "good." After all, aren't we all willing to look the other way or rationalize the mistreatment of others at times? It's okay as long as we aren't the ones being abused and we are getting what we want.

Remember the dopamine response that we all get when we get what we want, as well as the cortisol response when we are afraid? Those responses help to make Schindler believe that getting what he wants is good, despite his abuse of the workers to get it.

Stern does not celebrate with Schindler each time he is offered some small reward or pat on the back. He maintains his humanity, risking punishment if he is caught—and his use of the factory as a refuge is, of course, discovered. Fortunately, the person who discovers it is Schindler.

Schindler becomes confused and upset. He moves from the pleasure of getting everything he wants to the fear of loss. What if he gets caught? He can't be seen as a sympathizer; he would lose his reputation and all the money and prestige he has gained. Worse yet, he could lose his life.

Schindler gets caught in the dilemma between the two paths when he is confronted with an event that his greed can no longer justify. He has been witnessing the systematic execution of Jewish people in the camps. While out horseback riding with his latest mistress, he sees Jewish men, women, and children brutally and casually murdered—unless they can prove that they are able to work, and thus have value.

Schindler's workers haven't been harmed, so his business isn't affected, but he can no longer convince himself that his war profiteering is benign. Should he keep the money, the women, and the life of luxury, or risk everything to help his friend Stern save as many people as they can?

Ultimately, Schindler commits to the path of humanity, despite the risks. He has seen enough abuse and heard the German soldiers offer enough excuses for it. He can no longer justify the suffering and death of others who had been defined as the enemy—defined as less so that he could be more. He comes to a profound realization: all the money he has made, his status, and his reputation were brought about through abuse. Everything he has done for his own profit was a horror. His limited personal perspective and beliefs can no longer blind him to reality. His realization of the path of the justification of inhumanity brings him to his knees, and he decides to help Stern.

When he learns of the final order from the German high command, the extermination of all Jews in the work camps, Schindler vows to save as many Jewish workers as he can. His newest factory is making tank shells, so he decides to sabotage production. He pays to set up a camp away from areas under military control and send his workers there. To do so, he spends all the money he'd gained through their forced labor to buy special favors from various corrupt officials.

By choosing humanity over his desire for personal profit and the fear of losing his money, and even his life, Schindler connects to his truly human heart. He realizes that if he had only done this earlier, he could have saved many more lives. It's heartrending. We have all done this on a small or large scale. We have all let our desires outweigh our humanity.

ABUSE OF POWER:
THE THREE EXCUSES FOR ALL ABUSES

Liberty may be endangered by the abuse of liberty,
as well as by the abuse of power.
—James Madison

How can someone like Oscar Schindler knowingly cause the suffering of others for personal gain? How can that level of abuse even happen? The answer can be found by examining the oldest assumptions that run throughout our histories.

We are all born into man-made systems. They are all we have ever known as reality. What if those systems are already imposing a person's or group's limited perspectives, which violates the functional equality of the Golden Rule? What if that is why things have never been able to work? What if man has made these systems but has not realized the difference between the limited, selfish perspective and the functionality of the perspective of equality for the whole? Wouldn't it make sense, then, that the level of function or dysfunction correlates with the degree to which people have built systems that function equally for everyone—or only for the few?

Humans have come up with three main justifications for replacing the Golden Rule with their own personal ideas, three root excuses for all the abuses of man-unkind. These justifications have been around so long that they have become assumptions—the root legless chickens that determine how things have always been and how they always will be. We read or hear them in the news every day. We can see them in movies. They're in our music and our history books.

To hide our personal desires for gain and fears of loss and justify our true motivations, we humans have replaced the functional aspects of merit, justice, and stewardship with the concepts of ownership, laws, and money. All our systems are based on these concepts, which are fine within the confines of our personal, limited perspectives. We all need to learn by trial and error. But problems arise when we impose our personal beliefs on others.

This is just another way of describing the act of someone taking control. We know that control is a function of the wrong wolf, because that impulse comes from the fear of loss and the desire for personal gain, but no one can claim the right to control anything unless they can first claim ownership over it.

> *Power is of two kinds. One is obtained by the fear of*
> *punishment and the other by acts of love.*
> *Power based on love is a thousand times more*
> *effective and permanent than the one*
> *derived from fear of punishment.*
> —*Mahatma Gandhi*

The false belief is that if one owns something, one has the right to define that thing in their own image and use it however they see fit. Personal definition is key. Ownership gives the idea that we have a right to define, and we believe we own what we define.

The converse of that is also true. When someone defines a thing, they create personal conclusions and beliefs. That also gives us the sense that we own what we have defined as an extension of ourselves. We have defined it from our limited perspective and created a belief that we think is the truth. We own a belief that may not be true, and if we don't examine that legless chicken we can use it to give ourselves permission to do whatever we want with whatever and whoever we have created those beliefs about.

How do things work out when those who claim authority over others attempt to make their personal limited perspectives into laws or rules that all must follow? The excuse for every abuse starts with the claim that the man-made systems of ownership, laws, and money give people the "right" to do so. These three claims are woven together in any abusive narrative and are alive and well in the dysfunction of our systems today.

Because Oscar Schindler "owned" his Jewish workers, he thought he could do whatever he wished with them—for personal gain. He could even kill them if he wanted to. His success was not based on merit; he was deemed successful because of how much money he made by abusing others.

Can you see that people use their personal definitions and beliefs to justify their abuses? People have been taught to believe that if it's legal, it's not a crime, right? The keeping of slaves throughout history is common. What Schindler did was totally legal, according to the German authorities. Did a group of people declaring that abusing another group was legal make it right? This is an easy one—but I promise you, we were all taught that whatever we believe justifies whatever we do, without question or examination.

Every day, people use their personal beliefs to justify the imposition of their will through personal judgments, wars, violence, discrimination, murders, greed, and more. All of it comes from the limited perspectives of those who justify their actions with their personal definitions and desires to avoid loss and achieve personal gain.

Schindler did it for what he believed was personal profit. The officials that he bribed did it for personal gain. This desire for gain and the fear of loss, and the accompanying dopamine hit each time they got what they wanted, allowed and encouraged the Nazis to look past their own incredible inhumanity. They made a system and passed laws that said they essentially owned the Jewish prisoners. They gave themselves permission to do what they wanted by writing those laws, and they thought there was merit in it because they were making money. Are today's businesses any different? Do you see all the resulting problems that cascade outward into the larger society with each imposition of authority? Only the scale is different. Equality on a grand scale is a simple and direct indication of functionality.

If you believe the patterns that excuse man's abuses are found only in business and government, or only in certain instances or times throughout history, just look around you. These same patterns crop up in all our stories, both current and ancient. See if you can recognize the same patterns in the following ancient story from the book of John in the Christian tradition.

"Jesus went to the Mount of Olives. Now, early in the morning, He came again into the temple, and all the people came to Him; and He sat down and taught them. Then the scribes and Pharisees brought to

Him a woman caught in adultery. And when they had set her in their midst, they said to Him, 'Teacher, this woman was caught in adultery, in the very act. Now Moses, in the law, commanded us that such should be stoned. But what do You say?' This they said, testing Him, that they might have SOMETHING of which to accuse Him. But Jesus stooped down and wrote on the ground with His finger, as though He did not hear. So, when they continued asking Him, He raised Himself up and said to them, 'He who is without sin among you, let him throw a stone at her first.' And again, He stooped down and wrote on the ground. Then those who heard it, being convicted by their conscience, went out one by one, beginning with the oldest even to the last. And Jesus was left alone, and the woman standing in the midst. When Jesus had raised Himself up and saw only the woman, He said to her, 'Woman, where are those accusers of yours? Has no one condemned you?' She said, 'No one, Lord.' And Jesus said to her, 'Neither do I condemn you; go and sin no more.' Then Jesus spoke to them again, saying, 'I am the light of the world. He who follows Me shall not walk in darkness but have the light of life.'"

Does this story remind you of the Schindler's List example? Those who brought the woman to Jesus believed they had authority because they were from the church that wrote, and often enforced, what they had defined as "moral" laws. They believed they had the right to render judgment and punishments. This story is over 2,000 years old.

This woman was caught in the "very act" of adultery. That means she was caught having sex with someone who was not her husband. The legal punishment according to church law was death. This mob of strangers were planning to stone her to death. Do you think that group of people believed they had the right to kill her because of the permission granted by those in "authority?" Why would Jesus go against accepted authority?

Jesus taught that there were only two primary commandments to follow: love your God, which is what is true, with all your heart, soul, and mind; and love your neighbor as yourself. He reinforced those teachings by showing that there is another path, full of the desire to gain and a fear of loss. The path of mistaking the selfish perspective for the truth of the whole. He called following this path sin. Sin means to miss the mark—to make the mistake of replacing God, which is the universal functioning of the whole of reality, with the limited perspective. Imposing one's personal beliefs, interpretations, and conclusions without curiosity that there might be something more.

Jesus also said, "No servant can serve two masters; for either he will hate the one and love the other, or else he will be loyal to the one and despise the other. You cannot serve God and mammon."

No matter what any man-made system or person ever claims, they can never serve the path of humanity and the path of inhumanity at the same time. The two paths are mutually exclusive. No one can ever act based on their limited perspective and have that work for the whole. Man's imposed systems of money, ownership, and law do not create the equality that Jesus taught.

Since the child sexual abuse scandal in the Catholic Church first came to light in the 1980s, the Church has faced thousands of reported and verified cases of sexual abuse of children by priests, nuns, and others at various levels of the organization.

I listened to the public statements and interviews when this scandal first came to light. The scandals have gone on for decades, and accusations continue to be made by thousands of children, teens, and adults from parishes all over the world. I remember how dumbfounded I was when I heard an interview in which a Church spokesperson said that it was no one's business but the Church's, because the Church is self-governing; church and state are separate, and government law has no authority. Only the Church could decide if the priests had committed crimes, and the Church had forgiven the priests. They had no responsibility to address the suffering that they took part in creating.

Problem solved.

They could not admit that they had violated the Golden Rule by allowing the priests to impose their own will onto defenseless children, threatening them with consequences if they told anyone, and by redefining the teachings of their religion based on their own limited perspectives. They had made their own morality according to their own desires, changing "Thy will be done" to "My will be done."

> *Power tends to corrupt,*
> *and absolute power corrupts absolutely.*
> *—Lord Acton*

If you think the story of Schindler's List, or the 2,000-year-old story of Jesus at the Mount of Olives, or the above scandal from the 1980s are too far in the past to be relevant in today's world, I offer up two more movie examples that demonstrate these same patterns of abuse: *Erin Brockovich* and *The Big Short*. These two films reveal the exact same patterns for the justification of abuse: ownership, money, and law giving people special man-made rights to claim the power to do whatever they want, imposing their will for personal gain or the fear of personal loss, and the inevitable destruction that results.

Erin Brockovich is the true story of a single mother who, while looking for employment, wound up working for a lawyer. She noticed a pattern of illness in a town near an energy company and discovered that they were knowingly poisoning the people. Her persistence and humanity in the face of threats to her safety, as well as the army of lawyers sent to intimidate her and legally justify the abuse for profit, is a beautiful example of standing firm when faced with threat. The movie also shows that same justification of abuse by the corporation, the special "right" of individuals to use the same excuses to justify their actions.

When the corporation couldn't scare Erin off by threatening her personal safety, they brought out their lawyers to argue the "legal" rights of ownership and the privilege they thought they deserved due to their money, power, and importance—at the expense of the people they were poisoning because of their corporate greed.

Interestingly enough, the energy company's executives were never held personally accountable; the laws that corporations have lobbied Congress to pass protected them from personal liability.

In *The Big Short*, the financial industry's desire for profit led to massive irresponsibility on the part of banks and the government, ultimately leading to the global housing collapse in 2008. None of those who committed the massive fraud were personally punished, due to liability protection for corporations. Are you seeing the pattern yet?

Anyone who commits any abuse, does whatever they want regardless of the consequences, must circle back to these three excuses to justify their actions. They use these same excuses to avoid accepting any personal responsibility for the destruction that they took part in. They get all the rewards and none of the punishments—the goal of the limited, selfish perspective. All the pleasure and none of the pain.

In the beginning of *Schindler's List*, Schindler tells himself that he is not responsible for imposing his will on the workers. The party in power had imposed those laws during the war. He is benefiting from the laws, but he didn't write them. He didn't start the war. He doesn't abuse or mistreat the prisoners. It's okay because it's legal, and he would be a fool to pass up free labor. He is just trying to get rich, after all.

In the church scandal, the church didn't accept responsibility for the damage done to the abused children, whether it be financial, criminal, or personal. because they owned the definition of sin, they had the right of authority over the Bible, and they alone defined morality. They claimed to have no criminal liability because they weren't subject to the laws of nations, since the church and state are separate. Forgiving their priests meant that no crime had been committed. They "believed" they had that power.

In *Erin Brockovich*, the executives of the powerful energy company claimed that they weren't responsible for the operations of the plant—until their responsibility was proven by internal documents. After that, they brought out an army of lawyers to mitigate the financial loss without ever being held personally liable.

In *The Big Short*, the bankers thought they weren't responsible for the global crisis because all the other banks were selling the same fraudulent products, so they were just doing what they had to do for personal gain. All the financial devastation wasn't their fault. Why should they care about the consequences when they had liability protection? From their greedy perspective, it was a win-win. They not only got a taxpayer-funded bailout, they used it to give themselves big pay raises and bought property at a deep discount, in contrast to the millions worldwide who lost their life savings and homes.

There are endless examples of irresponsibility and inhumanity committed in the name of personal desire for gain and the fear of loss. In each case, someone's limited personal perspective is at the bottom of it—the belief that they have some special power stemming from the man-made systems of money, law, and ownership. And without exception, those impositions ripple outward and their destruction affects all of society.

But these patterns also apply to the perspective of the whole. The hero's journey. It's always a story in which someone has imposed their will on someone else, and the hero stands up for equality and sets things right. The hero restores the Golden Rule by ending the tyranny of one imposing their will onto another through threats and punishments. We all cheer when good triumphs in any story.

Interestingly, Jesus never preached punishments. In every recorded teaching, he only taught and lived the Golden Rule, following the true-hearted path of love and humanity. He never once imposed his opinion on anyone. He didn't try to remake God in his image; he saw everyone stuck in their limited, selfish perspectives. He knew they were missing the mark of humanity, and he helped each person to seek the larger perspective of truth. What can defining God be, other than personal interpretation? If we do that, are we not remaking "God" in our own image? Isn't that just another form of imposing one's will?

You can see the two paths in every movie. You can see it in every biography and every hero's journey. Movies like *Green Book*, *The Best of Enemies*, *The Last Samurai*, *Boy Erased*, and even one of my all-time favorites, *Kung Fu Panda*. The same patterns are even written into the United States Constitution.

In the Declaration of Independence, it is written that all men are created equal in the eyes of God. From that, it was asserted that all laws be just and equally applied. But another group who wrote part of the Constitution and the founding laws believed the exact opposite. They believed that they were justified by the rights of ownership, laws, and money, so the people were subject to whatever laws they passed and that their word was law.

Right there in the founding documents and the Constitution, we see both equality and inequality. All people being created equally in the eyes of their Creator, endowed with inalienable rights to life, liberty, and the pursuit of happiness, right next to those giving themselves special rights to violate the Golden Rule and impose their limited perspectives, making the rules everyone else should follow. After all, women and slaves were considered property. In the Constitution, this resulted in every Black person being defined as 3/5 of a person and women having no right to vote. Don't people have the "right" to do whatever they want with their own property? If something is legal, isn't it okay to do it?

THERE ARE ONLY TWO PATHS

The age-old, unexamined belief—that ownership equals authority, money equals merit, and law equals right—is still being used every day, all over the world, to take away the rights of others. Those in authority, business, and religion use it to give themselves permission to squelch free speech; it's why internet companies sell our private information instead of honoring our constitutional right to privacy. It's how governments justify laws that take more and more freedom away from the people. Not ironically, while doing all that, those in authority are constantly looking to expand exemptions for their actions. To get more liability protection.

Officials in government believe they aren't bound to serve the people; they own the "right" to write the laws. And the method they use to keep this concept alive is always the same. Whether it be marketing or politics, business or religion, they do it by taking advantage of people's personal fear of loss and desire for gain.

But belief isn't truth. Truth functions no matter what people believe. There is no belief required to easily recognize the imposition of will and how it violates equality. Where do all beliefs come from? All beliefs come from each individual's limited personal perspective.

We were all taught that people in authority are above us, but people are just people, regardless of their status or rank or what roles they fill. We were taught that some people are more important than others. Who taught us to believe that? The very people who create and control the systems. No one is exempt from the two paths and no position—high or low—reflects any person's level of humanity or understanding.

This has been the case throughout all of man's history. Those who impose their limited perspectives keep trying to overturn the universal functionality that is already built into a world that no business, government, or religious leader created.

MAN'S LAW VS. GOD'S LAW: PERSONAL, LIMITED BELIEFS IN PLACE OF FUNCTIONAL WISDOM

Now take a minute and slow down. God's law? What does that mean? Does that mean a return to church rule instead of government rule? Of course not. We have all been taught a bunch of things to believe about God and "His" rules and laws. Who made those up? Men did. Again, the limited perspectives of men trying to create definitions and make them true for the whole. That has certainly failed in an epic way throughout history.

We are taught that God is truth, right? Well, truth is an absolute, like functionality. Gravity works and is a constant that applies equally to everyone. Let's look at "God's law" as the way reality functions, without regard to anyone's personal beliefs. What if we lost the entire point of what was taught by all the so-called spiritual teachers, due to all the definitions and beliefs that we learned without ever examining the function underneath? Legless chickens, anyone?

If, in fact, we fulfill the Golden Rule through equality, then equality is required for things to function properly. If that is true, inequality is created by the imposition of will, which violates the Golden Rule, resulting in dysfunction.

Think about it. Can any crime be committed without someone imposing their will on others? Rape, murder, violence, theft, the rule of dictators, wars, and so on. For any "crime" there first must be an imposition of will. Are there any exceptions? If not, every crime requires the imposition of will, and that results in conflict.

EVIL BEGINS WHERE
EQUALITY ENDS

What about pure functionality in our systems? Do we need equal justice in all our courts of law, or should the richest person with the best lawyers win? Is that justice, or is that inequality based on ownership, laws, and money? What happens every time any person tries to make their personal, limited perspective more important than equal justice?

In the courts, when it's only a matter of money and not equal justice, people lose faith. When the police try to excuse the abuses of their officers who impose their personal ideas of "justice" instead of protecting and serving, people lose faith in the police. When governments pass laws to represent special interests, people lose faith in governments. The creation of inequality through the imposition of one's will over another is always a crime against humanity.

Isn't that the root of all our issues? Is it possible to make inequality functional when it is the very function of disrespecting others? Think about the moving parts of respect. Don't we need equality to fulfill respect? If you put yourself above someone, aren't you disrespecting them? Also, if you put yourself below someone, aren't you disrespecting yourself? Equality is absolutely required for the very functionality of respect.

Consider equality a universal truth like math. It is an absolute. 1 plus 1 always equals 2, right? In the same way, the universal function of equality always works until someone imposes their will and justifies any number of abuses with excuses based on their personal "right" to do so. Then, nothing adds up anymore. This is why the world is in the shape it is in.

For all our histories, we have been trying to make the limited perspectives of the few be the rules for the many, but no one can make inequality work. No one can make sin into truth. No one can make money into merit or law into justice. It is simply not possible to make evil into good. We will never make dysfunction function.

We think that when we grow up we stop playing make- believe, but all that happens is we learn to take our make- believe seriously. If you don't take what others tell you to believe seriously, you won't get into heaven. If you don't take the advice of businesspeople, you will never be financially free. If you don't follow the rules of the government, no matter how inhumane and ridiculous, you are breaking the law. And if you don't accept the ruling of the supreme court of the land, which says that corporations are actually people, you are in denial of reality.

But who, in fact, is denying reality? Does someone telling you that corporations are people align with reality, or are they playing make-believe? Does declaring that corporations are people make it true, or is that a fantastic belief with no basis in reality? Let's test it. Turn your head and cough, corporation. Well, it can't. It's literally a thing made up of words on a piece of paper. It's just people making up beliefs that they want to be true and telling us what to believe. Remember how we can easily believe that thoughts plus feels equals totally for reals?

This selfish nature seeks to remake the world in its own image, calling itself good while calling anything that it disagrees with evil.

Many of those people label themselves as authorities. People who have the right to impose their will over others. We see it every day in the media and in our politics, both in our country and worldwide. We are taught to believe that conforming to systems made by "authorities," without questioning them, is the way to make things work, but actually those systems can only fail if they are based on someone else's limited selfish perspective and not the functional wisdom of universal functionality that honors all people equally.

Why do we keep making the same mistakes over and over since the dawn of all histories? We have all tried to impose our beliefs on others and the world. We have all been deceived, believing that our definition of "good" is actual goodness. We have all done the judging and tried to impose our will on others and the world.

None of us want to hurt ourselves or others when we are on our true-hearted path. As the question from the scriptures goes, "Why do I do the evil that I don't want to do and not do the good that I want to do?" How can we keep mistaking what we call good for actual good? It is because of our personal Matrix of beliefs that are not our own but have been taught to us from birth.

CONFORMITY IS ABNORMALITY

Monkey see, Monkey do
—Anonymous

If you haven't heard about the five monkeys experiment, it goes something like this: A researcher puts five monkeys in a cage. In the cage there is a bunch of bananas hanging from a string, with a ladder leading to the bananas. When the first monkey goes for the bananas, the researcher sprays all five monkeys with freezing water for 5 minutes. Sometime later, when a second monkey inevitably tries to go for the bananas, the researcher once again sprays all five monkeys with the cold water for 5 minutes. The researcher then puts the hose away and never touches it again. But when a third monkey tries to go for the bananas, the other four attack him to prevent him from climbing that ladder. They are afraid of the punishment that they are sure will come.

Then, the researcher replaces one of the monkeys with a new monkey who wasn't part of the original experiment and was never sprayed with water. As soon as he touches the ladder to go for the bananas, the other four monkeys attack him to keep him from doing so. If he tries again, they attack him again. Thus, the new monkey learns not to go after the bananas because he will get attacked if he does.

The researcher replaces a second monkey with another new monkey. When this monkey goes for the bananas, the other four attack him, including the new monkey who was never sprayed with water. The researcher then continues to replace all the monkeys one at a time, until all five of the original monkeys are removed from the cage. Each time the newcomer goes for the bananas, the others attack, even when they, as new monkeys, have never received punishment for going after the bananas. All the new monkeys have learned not to go after the temptation of the bananas.

The researchers hypothesize that, if they asked the monkeys why they don't go for the bananas, they would answer "because that is how it has always been."

Now let's return to that scene from *The Matrix*. Do you remember that beautiful line that says the Matrix is the world pulled over your eyes to blind you to the truth?

This is exactly why so many believe that life is happening to them and not for them. Just like the five monkeys, we were born with natural instincts, an exuberance and joy for being alive and playing. Boundless curiosity and excitement. Just like the monkeys, however, we were trained with rewards and punishments not to trust our true nature. We were taught to replace truth with beliefs—the requirements and conditions of other people that we must meet before we can be free to enjoy the life that was once our baseline nature.

Over time, we have forgotten the reality of our true hearts and the magic of discovering the real world, so we conform. Everything becomes layer after layer of how to act and who to be to be acceptable to ourselves and others. We begin to believe we must fulfill those requirements to be free. Like the monkeys—their nature is to go after the bananas. There is nothing wrong with that nature, but through training, they quickly become afraid of their natural instincts and begin imposing their will on others to avoid the risk of pain, deferring to their masters in hopes that maybe, one day, they might get the banana.

Do you see that they now have a permanent problem? Their natural desire is to get that banana, and nature has supplied that banana freely until this experiment. But now they have been trained through punishments to stop going for the banana. I am sure that at least one of them would stare at it from time to time, wishing that one day they could have that banana.

Who is responsible for creating the problem for the monkeys and the resulting dysfunction when another monkey goes for the banana? Who creates the dysfunction—the person or group who imposes their will because they claim the right to, or the one they impose their will on? Was it the monkeys attacking the other monkeys or the researchers who first imposed their experiment on the monkeys?

The scientists are in control and the monkeys are being trained to conform. Would there even be a "problem" without the scientists' imposition of their will?

LOST IN THE ILLUSION OF REALITY

The use of punishments and rewards as a means to blind people to abuses is as old as history itself. If the monkeys asked the scientists why they did what they did, the scientists would say that they have a right to do to them whatever they want, no matter how cruel or unusual, because they own them. Just like Oscar Schindler and the ruling Nazi party did with the Jewish people. Just like the American slave owners did with their slaves. Just like companies do with their workers today. Just like any denomination of any religion or organization does in countless scandals. Pick any system in any country and do an internet search on abuses perpetrated by those in authority, and you will find them.

In all the cases listed above—Erin Brockovich, the global financial crisis, the church scandals, politicians lying to get into office and serving the corruption that got them there—the one thing that they have in common is that they only get rewarded. How can we ever expect anything to change when those in power have written laws that exempt them from any responsibility for their actions? If all it takes to exempt someone from something is to write new laws, what will change their behavior? If we reward the banks when they crash the global economy, if we reward corporations when they poison communities and politicians when they lie and cheat, and we bow to judges because they say they have the "rights" of authority granted by ownership, laws, and money, what are we doing besides encouraging more of the dysfunction they are creating?

This turns true humanity upside down and has created the insane fantasy that is now imposed upon us. We live in an age in which corporations are people and employees are not.

The root question is the same for all people, all systems, and all nations: Who is responsible for the societal dysfunction that results from the systems being imposed on everyone? Is it the citizen who won't follow the rules to make the system work for those who created it, or is it those who impose their will? Like the five monkeys, does the system work for the monkeys, or are the monkeys being forced to conform to the system? Who is being served, the people or the system? Without a doubt, the slave owner believes that the nonconformity of the slave is the problem.

Exactly like the problems in the world today, we have all been taught that we are responsible to solve the problems that surround us in society, and that they are not the result of the people imposing their will upon us.

We are taught that these are "moral" issues or "government" issues. Corporations tells us that they are "money" issues. But if you look at the big picture, all our problems arise from the imposed man-made systems of money, laws, and ownership, corrupted by the inequality created by the imposition of the limited, selfish perspectives of those corrupting them. All coming from their fear of personal loss and their desire for personal gain.

More important, we are taught that these problems can only be solved by conforming to the systems. If we want to be free, we must give up our freedom and conform to make the systems work.

Just as Schindler used the workers to serve his needs, just as the scientists trained the monkeys to attack the new monkeys, the people who run the systems are using their positions to corrupt the functionality of those systems.

This is the Matrix of belief that you, I, and everyone else is born into, but which cannot be made to function for anyone, no matter how hard we are forced to conform.

Do we really get to define good and evil—define reality in our own image—or is there a reality behind all of this creation that was alive and functioning perfectly before we got here, and will continue to function after we are gone? Did we create all of this or are we a part of something that created all of it?

We have all been taught to conform to abnormal systems and requirements placed upon us by other people. They are always sold to us as "better" or "for the greater good," but how can we know? Who is it better for? Would you have to force anyone to conform to a system if it truly functioned well for them? Wouldn't you choose a system that worked by personal choice if it was working for you?

Is the problem the bored, discouraged student, the overworked teacher, or the system imposed upon both of them? After all, what is the student's job but to conform to the goals set by the system? What is the teacher's job but to find a way to make the students conform? There was a time when a teacher's only job was to teach kids the tools they needed to explore the world—skills like reading, writing, and arithmetic. That used to be the banana. An educated, self-motivated society of people with equal opportunities who could pursue their own curiosity and knowledge and then be rewarded for their personal merits. Now, students and most people only get the banana if they conform to the system.

The issue at the heart of this is that we have all been taught that this is the norm. And this is how things will always be if we never inquire into reality. Since we have forgotten the reality behind the system, and the other four monkeys have convinced us to believe that this is how things have always been, we forget who is running the experiment that is creating the problems.

THE LEVEL OF ALL SOLUTIONS: THE POWER OF EQUALITY AND ENDING THE IMPOSITION OF WILL

I come not to abolish the law but to fulfill it.
—*Jesus of Nazareth*

What if this is the legless chicken that has never been examined? Can man define reality and make it conform to man-made systems instead of aligning with reality? Can someone's personal make-believe ever be reality? Can anyone make a system or situation from their limited perspective that will work for everyone? Are there requirements to make laws just? Can inequality ever be fair? What if we have lost sight of the functionality of truth due to the beliefs we've been taught since birth?

Maybe this is what is creating all the destruction in our lives and the world—everyone gone mad trying to make their personal fantasies about morality and reality "real" by imposing them onto the world, instead of aligning with a just world that already exists. Only if we understand that this false path is the root of all problems will we figure out that resolution can only come from the level that is not creating the problem.

TO HONOR OUR JOURNEY, WE MUST HONOR THE RIGHT OF EACH TO FREELY JOURNEY

The two paths can be summed up simply: they are the path of the limited selfish perspective and the path of the truth of functional reality. You can see the difference in the many examples I've offered, from Schindler to the monkeys.

The path of true functionality is what the spiritual teachers came to teach us. Jesus, the Buddha, and countless others have taught us that the love of money is the root of all evil. That is what we call greed. Remember that the path of truth is how things truly function. How does greed function? What makes a person greedy? Greed is a never-ending desire for more, a fear of not enough. It is the false path of the personal desire for gain and the fear of loss. Its only function is dysfunction. It always sacrifices the good of all on the altar of its personal perspective, using excuses rooted in personal ownership, money, and the influence to impose them through laws.

The functionality that is already built into the universe is objective and elegant, but for us to see it we have to look beyond what man has layered over it. To have all things function, we need to follow three simple and objective steps.

First, identify the root or initial imposition of will. It is always the ones in power who directly impose their will and justify their abuses or deputize others to do so. Anything that comes after that will be the result of the back-and-forth resistance to the imposition, and is secondary—not the root cause. If you drill down on the belief that any person or group uses to justify any imposition, you will find that their true motivation is their personal desire for gain and fear of loss.

Second, everyone—regardless of their claims of exemption or authority—MUST be held accountable fully, personally, financially, and criminally, for each and every imposition. Corporations are people, right? Well, even if that is not true, the people who work there are. So are governments. So is law enforcement. Individuals and institutions are absolutely responsible for their actions and those of their employees. This is vital, because without this accountability on all sides and in all cases, there is no justice and the destruction is passed on to the whole of society.

Lastly, reject the imposed will—whether it is a law, a business, or a morality. After all, they are not reality. The fact is that the world worked before these impositions that caused the dysfunction.

With this simple, elegant approach, all the worst qualities of man's greed are discouraged while merit, stewardship, and justice are restored. It is completely objective and fully honors truth, justice, and liberty equally for all. This is what the framers of the Constitution knew—and the scientists have trained us to forget.

What is even more amazing is that these simple steps also completely fulfill both primary teachings of the Golden Rule: treat your brother as you would be treated, and love the truth of function with all your heart, mind, and strength. The very next sentence of that scripture promises that if we live by these two primary rules, functionality will fulfill all laws, scriptures, businesses, governments, and relationships.

Remember that the key to all of this functionality is love. Just following rules or staying in your intellect won't work. If you are in your head, you are dead. Imagine a world full of people enlivened by their true-hearted passions, honoring each others' journeys equally, each responsible for their own action and individually response-able for their own journey, limited only by not imposing their will on anyone else.

THE TRUE-HEARTED PATH: MOVING FROM IMPOSITION TO THE FREEDOM OF POSSIBILITY

In 1943, a man named Abraham Maslow studied the dynamics of human nature and published his findings. He concluded that mankind could not evolve into true, spiritual human beings unless and until a hierarchy of needs was established. He simply identified what all people need to survive: food, clothing, shelter, fuel, and water. Sadly, given what has been done to the world since, we might have to include breathable air at some point.

How are all these needs met? Where do the food, the water, the materials to build homes, and the fuel come from? Earth. Our planet. How much does the planet charge us for supplying all that we need to survive? Absolutely nothing.

But man has imposed systems of money, ownership, and laws that deny access to these needs. This denial of needs is fundamental to the resulting dysfunction of the systems; it is at the root of all the issues we see on the daily news.

Here is an aspect that is worth thinking about: Remember the question of who is responsible for all the problems, the one imposing the system or those upon whom it is imposed? Do you remember how I explained in the earlier chapters that the fight-or-flight response, when not actually necessary, creates all the dysfunctional events and bad behaviors?

The degree to which these basic needs are denied determines if and when the fight-or-flight response is triggered. In time, this creates patterns in neurology and behavior. We then take those patterns out into the world.

By creating and imposing systems of money, laws, and ownership on the world, the authorities have given themselves excuses to deny people's ability to survive.

MONEY OVER MERIT

Instead of freedom, now there is money. You need to make money to buy food to survive. You need money to buy a home and pay your taxes on that home, as well as paying the bank that holds the mortgage to avoid being made homeless. And you have to pay for profit "market" value, which is five to ten times the actual cost of materials and labor. All these requirements were put in place by institutions created by man. To pay those who claim ownership over what they did not create. Money began as a simple form of exchange of value; now it has become what we trade our lives for. Money is a functional, simple means of exchange in its proper context, but when it is used as a means to control others through personal ownership—or denied to force servitude—no true good can come of it.

OWNERSHIP IN PLACE OF STEWARDSHIP

Which corporations created the land? Which governments or religious institutions created the water? None of them, but they claim ownership over all of it. If ownership equals authority, as the laws of man say, then logically, all they have to do to rule the world is control the hierarchy of needs. Otherwise, how would they get what they desire to gain and fear to lose? How else can someone justify the inhumanity of their imposition of will? Instead of everyone having equal and easy access to survival needs, those needs have been commoditized as a means of control. Money has become a means for some people to get everything they want by denying others what they need.

As I write this, countless numbers of patents have been filed, and more are filed every day, to replace what the earth has given freely—ever-expanding declarations of man's ownership. Genetically modified seeds to replace the seeds freely given by the earth, patents for new genetic alterations for lab-grown meats and the human genome. A handful of companies have bought most of the housing, and water rights have been sold to corporations by politicians.

Slow down and really think about it. What if you owned your home, had access to real, healthy food, clean air and water, and the fuel to make it all work? What if all those who did the work were well paid, and the earth, which offers us all the things we need to survive and thrive, was respected? How many government programs would be needed? How would the next banking crisis or the next government shutdown or the next man-made institutional crisis affect you? Do you think we would be ready to bail out the greedy banks again, the next time they fail? Well, to correct the abuses of the banks, the government did make them 10 times larger. That will teach them a lesson.

If your needs could be met at only the cost of those workers who plant the trees and harvest the lumber for homes and support the earth to provide the food, water, clothing, and shelter that we NEED, and not those who profit from it, how many people would go to work for the abusive bosses and the greedy corporations? Would you not be more relaxed and less stressed? Would you have more time for your family and friends and stop listening to the hollow promises of politicians, who always talk about helping families but never deliver?

This kind of system would honor humanity by providing the hierarchy of needs, paying those who did the work and paying for the actual cost of materials. We could restore the man-made systems to functional systems of merit in place of money, justice in place of law, and stewardship instead of ownership. We could automatically bring everything back into functional balance.

Once you had your survival needs met, being forced to work for the corporations would end. If workers weren't forced to work for a terrible boss, the bosses would no longer be able to deny workers a fair wage. They also wouldn't have any incentive to mistreat you, because you could choose to leave. The forced work would become an actual work force.

Businesses would value employees. They would be willing to pay for merit again, as it would become the valued commodity. The motivation of greed would die as businesses moved away from forcing workers to compete for their wages and started valuing the cooperation of workers and how they contribute to the business. That would replace the current denial system of wage suppression and the corporate goal of getting maximum profit for minimum quality and minimum wage. Workers would be merit-based and take pride in their work again.

Work would be brought into proper context. You would own your choice and be working for yourself. You could choose to work at a level that met your basic needs and provided the creature comforts you wanted. Your life and time would be yours again. It would relieve you of the responsibilities put upon everyone and give you the freedom to choose and respond. The freedom that the Constitution promised, but the systems have denied.

THOSE WHO ARE IMPOSING THE SYSTEMS ARE THE PROBLEM

In addition to equality, there is a second beautiful function in the Golden Rule: personal responsibility. You can't love your neighbor as you love yourself without it. Are you responsible for how someone else treats your neighbor, or only for your own actions?

Corporations are people!
—United States Supreme Court (paraphrased)

Is it really institutions that do things, or is it the people hiding behind those institutions? Do governments declare war and commit atrocities or is it the people who run them? What about corporations? Are they really people, or are they only being defined that way to protect those who stand to gain from that protection? Isn't it the same with the church, or any other institution, for that matter? Why, then, are they not held personally responsible?

How many more corporate scandals would there be if their executives had to pay for them personally? How would things be different if they were personally, criminally, and financially responsible for their actions? Who do you think wrote the laws to exempt them in the first place? How many wars would there be if those who started them were held personally responsible to prove the need for war and personally risk their own assets and freedoms? How many media sources would knowingly print falsehoods if they were personally liable when the truth came out? How many politicians would pass laws for personal gain by trading legislation that creates more and more inequality in exchange for reelection donations and corporate jobs after they leave office, if they would be held personally responsible for their corruption?

If everyone was held equally responsible for their impositions, the environment would suddenly get a lot cleaner, because those who made the mess would be expected to clean it up. Do a quick internet search for superfund sites and see how the excuses of money, laws, and ownership are resulting in more billions of taxpayer dollars being used to clean up corporate sites so toxic that they claim they can't afford to pay for it themselves. They do, however, keep all the "profits." Ask yourself, is that creating more problems or is it solving them? Is that coming from the level that only creates more problems or the level of solutions?

The excuse corporations use is that they create jobs. Jobs support the economy and provide people with what they need to live. That is entirely false. People need the hierarchy of needs to survive. Food, clothing, shelter, water, and fuel. Money, ownership, and laws are the man-made excuses that deny them.

To restore everything back to balance, how about we just supply the hierarchy of needs at its actual cost, paying those who do the work, sharing what the earth has given freely, and not allowing anyone to deny access to anyone else for profit's sake by saying that they "own" what they didn't create?

> *The more laws and restrictions there are, the poorer*
> *people become. The more rules and regulations, the*
> *more thieves and robbers.*
> —*Lao Tzu*

But wait, a group of people in robes has declared that corporations are people, so it must be true, right? What impact would equality and the Golden Rule have on the courts? Equal justice would return to the courts, as they would no longer base all their decisions on their limited perspectives and opinions but would simply look at who was imposing their will and hold that person personally accountable for their crime—both financially and criminally. Is that not equal justice for all?

We are lost in our limited perspectives of belief. We believe in place of reality. Reality can only be found by first removing any overlay created by man. Mankind has forgotten that by some unknown means, this world and all the people in it are part of a creation that we had no part in creating. What part did we have in making the seasons or the intricate ecosystem for growing the food? No person or group of people made this world, and it functions according to the wisdom that sustains it. It functions from the whole of reality and is not based on how people or systems define it. Like the function of gravity, equality applies to all in reality.

ALPHA AND OMEGA

> *Our power is in our ability to decide.*
> —*Buckminster Fuller*

In the end, we are as we began. We were born into a childhood of disempowerment. We were empowered or disempowered by the parents and societies who defined us. We grew up and went out into a world that, as a result, is defined by us. We aren't aware that the world is already an illusory world imposed upon us from the moment we are born into it.

When I tell you that the only problem that you, I, or any person in the world has is that we mistake our limited perspectives for the whole of reality and believe negative emotions can lead to positive outcomes, resulting in the impositions of will, what do you think that means? When you judge yourself, who did you learn that from? Is that not the imposition of will from your parents while growing up?

When we judge others, where does that come from? When the courts, the politicians, or the billionaires use man's laws to justify the imposition of will and create inequality and more problems, don't you see it is because they don't realize they are acting based on their limited perspectives, which arise from their desire for gain and fear of loss? Oscar Schindler, the greedy corporations that silenced Erin Brockovich, the banks that created the global housing collapse, and the church that tried to bury its scandals are all examples of this. When ownership equals authority, no beliefs are examined, and assumption is the rule, it's all just legless chickens, imposed by the scientists who are creating the beliefs and norms for the five monkeys to carry out in society.

Can you think of a case in which the imposition of will isn't the basis for a crime? Can you find an example where equality wouldn't function perfectly in all situations? Then consider this: It is only when people move equality from function to concept and begin defining it from their personal perspectives that it doesn't function. It works perfectly in reality, but if replaced by personal belief it will fail.

WE HAVE TO LIVE THE GOLDEN RULE
FROM LOVE FOR THINGS TO WORK

The wisdom teachers taught a different path: the higher path of humanity and functionality. More important, they lived what they taught. They didn't just believe or disbelieve in concepts. Jesus had only two primary teachings: the Golden Rule and to love the truth with all your heart, soul, and mind. He taught equality for all matters of the mind. It is a way to universal logic.

Jesus gave us an objective measure for our hearts and minds and God gave us all the same gift—the gift of life, freely given for us to share and experience this creation. God is just a word. Whatever intelligence all of this came out of, words cannot capture it. They can only define it. They can be a shadow cast from the sun. They are fingers pointing at the moon; they are not the moon.

ACTUAL REALITY

Everything in life comes down to one question. A question for which we all have been given the wrong answer. We have been told that the way to freedom is through conformity to someone else's definitions.

When you look at actual reality, everything is unique. Each person's DNA, our voiceprints, our fingerprints, our journeys, our experiences. None of them are ever exactly the same as those of anyone who is living or has ever lived.

The question is, are you going to live freely and honor the life given to you by some creative force and intelligence that none of us created, or are you going to be defined by the limitations put upon you by others? Are you going to own your life fully, or are you going to spend your life trying to be right? Are you going to live what all the spiritual teachers taught, or are you just going to believe that you are better than those who disagree with you? In reality, everything about your life is your choice. All the problems that we see in the world are the result of our past choices, what we have chosen to settle for. We can change things as soon as we all change our minds, but we are going to have to stop choosing sides, stand for equality, and stop anyone from imposing their will.

None of this matters if we don't live it. No matter how many Schindlers, how many scandals, how many supreme court decisions or broken promises of politicians in all the histories of the world, nothing will ever change unless we apply the tools of equality and love. They will never be a part of you until you stop telling yourself that you understand them as a concept and start embodying them in every aspect of your life. This is a truth that will set you free.

What if we all loved the gift of universal functional truth with all our hearts, minds, and souls, instead of loving our limited selfish perspectives and the man-made systems of money, laws, and ownership? What if all we need to do is honor the Golden Rule and have a truly loving heart to be moral?

The only thing I am offering is the gift of objective truth. It is not mine. It can't be owned or defined by anyone. It is simply what Jesus and all true wisdom teachers taught as the functional reality of all creation. No one can give anyone the truth by words alone.

These are the tools that will show you the rest if you use them. An objective measure that fulfills all laws, all merit, and all situations, if you start living in the world of functionality and not belief alone. If we stop imposing our will onto the world in thought, word, and deed and start treating others as we would be treated.

Do you really think that if we just keep passing more laws, creating more programs, printing more money, or backing another political candidate or party, we are going to change any of the systems that are creating the problems?

We will all have to be part of the change. We have to bring equality and personal responsibility back if we truly want to see how great a world based in humanity, brotherhood, sisterhood, kindness, and patience would be to live and love in. Everything that will ever be right or wrong with the world depends on what path each of us chooses, whether we accept it with open hearts and minds or deny it by embracing the human creations of ownership in place of stewardship, money in place of merit, and laws replacing justice.

All of Life Is a Gift:
We Must Actually Live It

Many journeys, one path, many stories, same emotions.
Many perspectives, one truth.
—Steven Fidler

WHAT DO YOU THINK LIFE IS ABOUT? A big question deserves a pause to think about it. If all the information given in this book is real and functional, you, I, and everyone else have only two paths. The path of the limited, selfish perspective, deceptively fueled by negative emotions of the desire for pleasure and the avoidance of pain, or the path of true-hearted humanity fueled by love, patience, and kindness. The selfish path will always be petty, frustrated, and small, but if we get hung up on trying to make it work, we can get stuck in the pattern that can never work.

We can try—as we were all taught—to spend our entire lives trying to justify and verify every personal opinion and conclusion, imposing endless judgments on ourselves and the world. We can continue giving ourselves and others permission to abuse and punish, based on whatever rules, laws, or beliefs we wish to affirm as good or right, trying to make them true. We can continue with the endless rationalizations about how this is just the way things are, or should be, in politics, or that our personal morality is God's morality and we are just executing the will of God.

We can continue the cycles of destruction, all of which come from man's total disregard for the path of reality and love. We can keep trying to make this lie truth, or we can simply align with a truth that none of us created. We can use the Golden Rule as our guide and the heart of love as the foundation. We can stop pretending to know everything and simply get curious. We can stop judging and start inquiring. Stop labeling everyone and everything in our own image. More than all that, we can stop believing that we know the world just because we have been taught to define and judge the people and events in it.

A teacher once said something to me that, at the time, I didn't realize was not only a summation of the two paths, but also a truth: "We can be right, or we can be happy."

THE GREAT MYSTERY

If you really want to get back in touch with the mystery and magic of this world, ask yourself honestly: Who made it? Who made this world that is in ceaseless motion? Every atom and molecule shifting, pulsing, and vibrating with life in every moment and for all eternity. How does this ceaseless, perpetual, ongoing creation occur?

It is in and of all things. It is staggering to imagine that we have around 40 trillion cells in our bodies, all of which are doing tasks. Without our conscious effort, every cell in our bodies is creating, sustaining, coordinating, and dissolving all the functions to support life. Really think about that—40 trillion cells working in harmony, without input from any of us. Combine that with a complex ecosystem that produces all the food, water, and natural resources and a sun that sustains it. All of that created and sustained without us doing anything. It is mind-blowing.

Yet, we want to own it all. We want to define everything and make it ours. We really don't understand the depth of the mystery we are immersed in, and as we have developed habits and beliefs we have anesthetized ourselves to the wonder that we are a part of. What if the truth of all things is true, whether we agree or disagree with it?

Let's go through a bit of the science that we may have been taught to ignore because it doesn't affirm what we want to believe. Have you heard about the aura? The idea that a colorful cocoon of energy surrounds each of us? Well, science has now developed the tools to measure and photograph it. What once was dismissed as superstitious nonsense by science, medicine, and religious institutions is now verifiably true.

The aura has been relabeled, of course. It has been given a new name, so that—since it is new to those "experts" who threw it out as nonsense—they don't have to admit they were wrong, and they call it a "breakthrough." Forget that it was a commonly known quantity in ancient times. The biofield—as it is now called—is a "new discovery."

If you want to see it with your own eyes, just do an internet search for Kirlian photography. That photographic style has also been adapted for video cameras, and I am sure that you can see video of the auras that surround people, if you so choose.

What else, then, might not be fully known in the world if auras now exist? Maybe this is a better question: Does labeling auras as superstitious spiritualism make them not real if science and religious institutions deny their existence? Is something true because people agree or disagree with it, or does reality exist regardless of beliefs?

Have you ever heard of remote viewing? The idea is that you can view remote places when you go into a meditative state. Look it up and you will read that there is no scientific evidence that it exists. The United States government funded a full study of remote viewers and only recently went public with the results. The data they collected—the actual data, not based on whether we like or dislike the idea—showed that those remote viewers' accuracy levels far outperformed the rate of random chance.

Most people still believe that life is what we choose to believe in or deny. What makes something feel true to us is simply whether we agree with it or not. That is all coming from our personal, limited perspectives. The truth really doesn't care about opinions. The truth simply is.

Belief is powerful, though. If you have heard of the placebo effect, you already know that. One thing I love about the placebo effect is that science uses it as a way of declaring outcomes of studies as unscientific, while it is the most consistent, scientifically validated effect ever studied.

The placebo effect is basically the impact that belief has on outcomes in controlled environments. For instance, when drug companies make a new drug, they have to outperform the placebo effect. To measure this, they set up one group of people who get the trial drug, and a second group who only get a sugar pill—a placebo. A substance with no physiological effect. The fascinating thing is that the placebo group is the group considered to be the invalidating group that the drug is to outperform. No scientist ever says, "WOW! Look at the impact of the body when the mind believes! Maybe we should study how to enhance that instead of the drug."

The irony is that the placebo effect is responsible for around a 30 percent impact. That means if someone believes that they are taking a drug that lowers blood pressure, the placebo group will have up to a 30 percent impact as a result of their belief that they are taking the drug.

But it's not just with drugs. People who visualize vividly create similar effects through belief alone. The placebo effect, therefore, is one of the most scientifically validated things in existence. It is evidence for the incredible power of belief, but belief can be used to harm or heal. It forms all our neurological patterns and the patterns in our physical bodies.

Now, remember that the two paths are always active within us all. Remember that we are constantly building and reinforcing neurological circuits. The brain doesn't have morality. Our neurology doesn't understand anything. It can only do what it is designed to do. It builds a support structure around our choices. Whatever we choose and wherever we put our attention, that's what builds our neurology. That includes our biases.

We don't realize that there is trauma stuck in our brains and our nervous system patterns. That's the real problem, not an inherent character weakness or a "wrong" attitude.

The good news is that neurology builds in both directions. Practice makes perfect and imperfect. The solution also lies within our brains and neurologies. These aren't fixed, immovable structures. They can be changed by trauma and reclaimed through neural exercises. That is the reality of neuroplasticity.

All our life choices are double-edged swords. They can be used to cut our bonds or to enslave ourselves and others. You have felt the power of negative emotions to wash away your humanity instantly, the same as I have. How easy, then, do you think it is to simply forget the path of love and kindness when we feed the neurology of judgments and negativity? How easy is it to look the other way or to judge and punish in place of a deep understanding that we all have the same two paths inside of us?

Did you know that there is something at the core of science called the measurement paradox? Similar to placebo, the measurement paradox shows that by simply observing an experiment at the subatomic level, we change its outcome. Think about those implications. Similar to our internal biases, whatever we expect to find influences the outcome. The observer and the experiment are connected. It is quite similar to which question you ask. Are you looking for reality or trying to verify your personal limited beliefs?

The measurement paradox, as well as biases, give us something to consider. How can we make this all work? If everything, even in the most controlled of circumstances—such as in a laboratory—is overturned by observation, and messy, noisy, day-to-day living is overthrown by personal biases, how can we find reality? Can the imposition of will ever be the answer?

This one thing is the entire reason that compelled me to write this book. The Golden Rule is taught by every wisdom teacher from every true spiritual practice. Always travel on the path of love, whether it is love for your neighbor or yourself or God. All the spiritual teachers lived by these tenets, and those who violate them are always falling back into their personal limited perspectives, self-verified and justified by the personal fear of loss and desire for gain, which only create more dysfunction and destruction.

> *My yoke is easy and my burden is light.*
> *—Jesus of Nazareth*

If Jesus taught that there were only two teachings above all others to live by—the Golden Rule and to love the truth with all your heart, soul, and mind—maybe we need an objective measure to keep things simple enough to make things work. We have to be able to live all of this. If we can't live it and only think about it, it is just empty words. Never yet to this point in our histories have we used this wisdom teaching, but we always have the possibility to change. In every moment, we can wake up to reality and align with the miracle of the life within and all around us.

We are all on a journey of realization through pain and failure. We're playing a game of hide and seek. Until we both individually and collectively understand the difference between the two paths, we will have to learn the hard way. We will continue to feed the wrong wolf, dance with the legless chicken, and fight with the monkeys about the bananas. Until we install the Golden Rule and come from the truly human heart of love and the functionality provided by not imposing our will on anyone else, we are in for more of the same.

It all goes back to Einstein's statement that you can never solve a problem from the level that creates it. All problems are created by the misappropriated use of the fight, flight, and freeze mind. All our systems were imposed from that mindset.

In all things, the only true power that anyone has is choice. The fact that we are born into a massive mess of laws, rules, and moralities, and we all cling to our personal beliefs, just confuses things. The other statement that I am reminded of is that the definition of insanity is repeating the same action over and over, expecting a different outcome.

We were born into confusion. We are the prisoners in Plato's cave naming the shadows on the wall, believing them to be reality. Then, we are taught that somehow, we have to make this lie true. So, we enter into hundreds and thousands of interactions in which we affirm or deny our beliefs and the beliefs of others, thinking that we are going to find the truth, but all we are doing is naming the shadows on our cave walls. To find the truth, regardless of what we believe, we must leave the cave.

Unity is realizing that we can all fall victim to the wrong wolf, but we also all have the capacity for true humanity. It is we who limit or expand the possibilities for both. The expansion or limitation depends on the level of tension or relaxation in the mind and body. The presence of the fight-or-flight response, or the level of relaxation and trust. None of it is complicated; it's simply a matter of life and death.

THE ROOT OF ALL SURVIVAL: LIFE AND DEATH

The sole purpose of the survival mind is to not die. To live forever. The fight-or-flight response, however, is a hard-wired response of the physical structures of the body. How can you make a body, which will ultimately fail, live forever? We all have to deal with this very conundrum.

The fight-or-flight mind is trying to save itself and make itself eternal, but so far, there is simply no way for the body to live forever. That is the realm of the soul and spirit. The ultimate mistake this survival instinct makes is trying to override the reality of the intelligence all around us to live forever, instead of aligning with life itself.

Look around you. Look at the world. Look at nature. Better yet, close your eyes and go inside. Look at your body. This world, with all of its systems and seasons, functions effortlessly.

Every year, we can see the cycles of life. Spring is birth, summer is the full flower of life, fall is the fading of that intensity into a richness of color and softer beauty, and winter finishes the cycle by allowing for rest. A time of pause before the cycle begins again.

There is a cycle in each day, as well. We have the birth of the day at sunrise, the spring of the day in the morning and early afternoon, the fall of the day into evening, and the darkness of night as the sun sets. Who or what designed this world in which all the seasons, the mountains and rivers, and the air that we breathe coalesce into what sustains all our lives, even as our bodies' trillions of cells support our life processes effortlessly? All of that, while mirroring back to us the cycles of death and rebirth in every day and the yearly cycle of the seasons!

Which government or corporation created this intelligence? Which then is sovereign? Did this intelligence exist before we were even here, or do we, by defining or labeling it from our limited perspectives with our thoughts and our conclusions, somehow make it work? Did things already function regardless of whatever we impose onto reality? We are born into a great mystery, sustained by some organizing principle or intelligence that we simply don't understand. The function of everything is so beautiful, in fact, that we don't even acknowledge it.

THE PATH OF TRUE REALITY IS THE PATH OF BEAUTY

You cannot do a kindness too soon,
for you never know how soon it will be too late.
—Ralph Waldo Emerson

To feed the real human heart, we can no longer turn to man's definitions. We will have to let go of the idea that by reading the theories and definitions of others and thinking, we are practicing these things. Remember, we can't earn a black belt in karate by reading about it or thinking about it; we have to practice it. We each have to find out for ourselves, through our own life experiences.

In the living and dying of life, death is the root of all fear. All the living that we wish we did or want to do, but don't, is rooted in the fear of not being able to survive if we follow our true humanity.

Take heart. None of us can claim to have created this world, but being taught from birth about the definitions and man-made systems of ownership, laws, and money, we can be deceived into believing that those things matter more than how we treat other people or ourselves.

Reality doesn't care about personal definitions, though. There is evidence in reality's patterns. Maybe the ever-repeating cycles of the seasons and the days aren't just cycles, maybe they are how things work. If the cycles of birth and death are represented in the seasons, and even the progression of each day, maybe there is no ending. Maybe there are only cycles of life and rebirth.

Fortunately, there is science to support this as well. There is evidence that these cycles of rebirth are going on not only around us, but inside of us as well.

There is an entire field of study called near-death experiences—the experiences of people who were considered dead according to science and medicine's current definitions. People whose bodies or minds have deteriorated enough to be clinically pronounced dead or are in such a state as to be irreversibly damaged have come back. Not only have they survived, but they have made full recoveries, which the experts thought was impossible.

I will mention three of my favorite examples: Dr. Jill Bolte Taylor, Dr. Ebon Alexander, and Anita Moorjani.

Dr. Taylor had a massive stroke. Her conscious awareness watched as her brain collapsed into total dysfunction. This level of damage ends in death for most people who suffer a stroke of this magnitude, but she lived. Of those who do survive, most have very serious residual effects. Most have extremely impaired function in their day-to-day lives. But Dr. Taylor made a total recovery. You can read her amazing story in her book *My Stroke of Insight*.

Dr. Ebon Alexander was a very accomplished practicing neurosurgeon when he suffered a severe brain infection, which damaged his brain so thoroughly that, by all accounts, he should have died. Technically, he did die, but he returned and brought with him all his experiences of a realm that we don't understand. He also should have had damage that could not be repaired, yet it was. Dr. Alexander made a full recovery. You can read his account in his book *Proof of Heaven*.

Then there is the story of Anita Moorjani. She had end-stage cancer that had spread throughout her entire body. She was on her death bed. Like Dr. Alexander, she had a curious experience of a strange realm when she was technically dead and then returned—and not just to finish out her last few days. To the astonishment of her doctors, she was in full remission from her cancer and made a full recovery. She is still with us today.

In science, it only takes three cases to establish a viable pattern. There are literally thousands more cases, not only of an afterlife but of reincarnation. The University of Virginia has a database of verified cases of 2,500 children who have had vivid memories of past lives, many of which have been corroborated as genuine. You can check that out here at this link if you are curious: UVADOPS.org.

I especially love biographies, because they show us what is possible despite what others have defined or taught us to believe is impossible. For years, it was believed that no one could run a 4-minute mile. It was believed so widely that people just assumed it was true. In 1954, Roger Bannister broke the 4-minute mile record. Shortly after he showed that it was possible, shattering that old limiting belief, others broke it as well. All our fields of medicine, politics, science, religion, economics, and even mathematics have been limited by those who have decided that, since they have not found a solution, there cannot be one. Rather than admit that they have not been able to find a way, they deny that anyone can find a way. We are conditioned to just believe and limit the possibilities in life. Worse yet, we are taught—like the five monkeys—to impose those beliefs on others.

You can see the same pattern in the following biographies and people's stories: *Bleed for This, The Walk, Cinderella Man, Miracles from Heaven, Hacksaw Ridge, and Wild.* You can see it by looking up other people who have done supposedly impossible things, such as David Goggins, Wim Hof, and yes, Jesus of Nazareth. These people didn't conform to the norms; they sought more than the standard accepted beliefs of their times and cultures. They found the truth through their own experiences.

All of these are stories about people who didn't let conformity and the definitions of experts stop them from choosing their lives. Solutions can never come from the level of the problems that are creating them.

The key with all this information is possibilities. What if we don't know everything? What if it's more like we don't really know much of anything? What if we learn how things work by exploring their dynamics and function, not by defining them or accepting someone else's explanation? What if the world really is run by an intelligence that does everything effortlessly for our sake? Not doling out punishments or rewards, but offering a constant invitation to align with that intelligence. An option to move from the temporary, false premise of the fearful survival-mind to an eternity that is always present, right now.

As I've mentioned throughout this book, I have realized many things, thanks to my journey, and one of the more interesting universal truths is that there is only NOW.

Think about it. When is it ever not right now? There is nothing else but now. Whether we are thinking about or planning for the future or remembering past events, we are always doing it right now. So past and future really are not places where anything is happening. We can only imagine future events and remember past events. They are both functions of how we use our imagination.

It's like that great saying, "The past is history, the future is a mystery, and the present is a gift; that is why they call it the present." If you examine the implications of this idea, the verifiable truth that it is always only right now, what does that imply? What if we are already living in eternity and have a choice—to align with it or deny it?

There are so many other wonders, so many fascinating and inspiring realizations, and so much to discover about this mystery that we are born into.

The true path is a path of beauty. A path of awakening. The path of now. It is a ceaseless movement of creation and destruction to create room again for new creation. A quiet expression of the formless taking form, moving back into formlessness. It is best found in the silence offered by true beauty. True art.

What if we are eternal souls living in temporary bodies? How could we be afraid about survival if we knew by direct experience that we were already eternal? That is the gift of all of life. The punchline to the Mona Lisa smile. Once we journey enough, we will realize that no matter how many times we try to gain favor with others, to get that money, that status, that relationship, or that castle to build our empire on, it will never get us to our true humanity. There is only one true power that we all are given equally by life itself: choice. Whether we choose to live from a heart of love or from the worry and hurry of the never-ending requirements of others.

YOUR CHOICE IS YOUR TRUE POWER

Kindness is more important than wisdom, and the
recognition of this is the beginning of wisdom.
—Theodore Isaac Rubin

We are all taught that there are mountains of things we must fulfill before things can work, before we can be free. In reality, we can all be free, regardless of the impositions of others.

Everything inside of us and around us in the world reflects what we have already chosen. The way we view the world is based on the neurology that we have fed by each choice we have made along the way, but we know we can change the neurology we have created through neuroplasticity.

By belief alone, we know that the placebo effect gives each of us a measurable 30 percent effect. That 30 percent will either get us 30 percent closer to free or 30 percent deeper into the illusion that we are not already free.

Our lives, these systems, and everything in this world will be determined by how we use our choices. We can run with the legless chickens or join the rabble of rabid monkeys. We can feed that fearful wolf until our neurology is built up enough that we are truly lost in our fears. We can feed that anger until we justify any level of abuse.

If we follow the path of the fear of personal loss and the desire for personal gain, perhaps we can be a king. Maybe more than a king. Maybe we can be the emperor of the whole world. Maybe we can set rules and requirements and make all of those around us serve us. Then we will have all we ever wanted—except for the love, peace, kindness, and humanity that make life worth living. We can believe that our crimes are not criminal until that illusion is burst by reality. It's all our choice.

> *If we let go of our personal, limited self,*
> *what we'll find is that love cures the heart and*
> *the Golden Rule, the mind.*
> —*Your author*

STOP MASTER DEBATING OR YOU WILL GO BLIND!

I love creative and playful things, so I couldn't resist. There is an old wives' tale that says if you masturbate too much you will go blind. Since we now know that there are only the two paths of objective truth and the limited perspective, there is no reason to debate. We have an objective truth that we can use. The only crime is the imposition of will and the only justice is equality. We can all stop debating, because it makes us go blind to the fact that we are debating from our limited perspectives when we get confused or upset. Relax, get curious. Then there is no more debate, only a synergy-seeking higher understanding.

But wait! What if this is all just my opinion, you say? Good question. What is the difference between an opinion and an objective measure? Why, it's the imposition of will, of course.

Where is the imposition of one's will on another from equality? Where are the negative emotions of the fear of loss and/or the desire for gain from equality? It's not my personal opinion, because it isn't about me. It's about everyone equally. That is why we have to stop master debating.

As soon as we get upset in any debate or impose a personal belief on someone else, both we and the person that we are debating instantly go blind to the fact that we are both debating from our limited perspectives. We forget that we are just people who are angry or scared, and it has impaired our judgment by making us up to 30 IQ points dumber. It is an unnecessary and unproductive tug of war that keeps both people captive.

> *There is no need for temples;*
> *no need for complicated philosophy.*
> *Our own brain, our own heart is our temple.*
> *The philosophy is kindness.*
> —*Dalai Lama XIV*

Instead, we can set ourselves and others free by restoring our right and the right of all to journey as we freely choose. We can stand up and dive into the mystery that is constantly unfolding around and inside us all, using the Golden Rule and the heart of love as our guide. We can only fulfill it by living the teachings of all the wisdom teachers. Nothing else will ever work.

We must stop just believing and start living our beliefs to take them from concepts to realities. If there is a God, how do you think we are going to find out other than by direct experience? Like believing or disbelieving in auras, or whether people get into heaven or go to hell based only on what they believe, we must stop master debating and learn through experience.

If there is an afterlife and a heaven, do we just "wish" ourselves there? If we believe hard enough, will that make it true? Maybe by simply labeling ourselves with some religious affiliation we will automatically get in, regardless of the actual state of our heart and mind?

If we are all limitless spiritual beings in the illusion of the temporary body, weren't we always fully free? Weren't we always eternal? Not blinded by belief, or mistaking our limited perspectives for the whole of reality. Instead, already living in the eternal, but now with the possibility of realizing the higher reality that we are a part of but did not create.

The Kingdom of Heaven is at hand.
—Jesus of Nazareth

"The Kingdom of Heaven is at hand," Jesus said. He also said that we have to "die to self" before we can enter the Kingdom of Heaven. What if the Kingdom of Heaven is all around us, but to see it we must develop the capacity to see reality behind what has been imposed upon it? Which "self" do you think must die—the loving one? The path of true humanity, or the selfish, judging, defining, labeling self? The fearful, petty, angry self?

From the path of love, Jesus promised eternal life. All true wisdom teachers taught the same. All true spiritual traditions also promise gifts that come by aligning with truth. Jesus healed people and brought back the dead. He walked on water and calmed the weather. Masters in the Buddhist traditions promised and did similar things. It is said that all things are possible when we are aligned with life itself. Jesus even promised that any who embodied and lived his teachings would perform all his miracles and more. We can't live any teachings from love when we are angry or afraid.

It takes great courage to face our fears, as well as to forgive our anger. There is no end to this journey, there is only a new beginning. Perhaps we can journey more together. Perhaps this is our end. Either way, it has been my pleasure to share with you and offer all this to you for your consideration. What happens now is your choice alone.

The last thing I want to leave with you is a recommendation to read the Golden Rule and the passage on love from I Corinthians in a new way—with eyes that see and ears that hear, after all we have shared together. Notice what you can and see if you can identify the comparison of the two paths, remembering that one is the limited perspective of the self and the other is the higher path of wisdom, true function, and humanity. The path that honors all equally. Where the duality ends. There are no winners or losers. We are all part of a learning, growing tapestry of life. The only way to follow this path is to recognize both paths and embrace the true-hearted humanity of love.

HERE IS A REMINDER ABOUT THE GOLDEN RULE:

1. In the Talmud of the Jewish tradition, the sage Hillel said: "What is hateful to you, do not do to others. This is the whole of the Law; all the rest is commentary."
2. In the Hindu legend of the Mahabharata, the divine Krishna declared: "This is the sum of duty. Do nothing unto others which would cause you pain if done to you."
3. In the Gospel of Matthew in the Christian scriptures, the messiah Jesus says: "Whatever you wish that others would to you, do also for them, for this is the Law and the Prophets."
4. In the Buddhist text of the Udanavarga, the student is urged: "Hurt not others in ways that you yourself would find hurtful."
5. In the Muslim Hadith of al Nawawi, the prophet Mohammed teaches: "No one of you is a believer until he desires for his brother that which he desires for himself."
6. In the T'ai Shang treatise of Taoism, the seeker is instructed: "Regard your neighbor's gain as your own gain, and your neighbor's loss as your own loss."
7. In the ancient wisdom of Shinto, there is a saying: "The heart of the person before you is a mirror. See there your own form."
8. The Oglala Lakota spiritual leader Black Elk wrote: "All things are our relatives; what we do to everything, we do to ourselves."

LOVE:

If I speak in the tongues of men or of angels but do not have Love,
I am only a resounding gong or a clanging cymbal.
If I have the gift of prophecy and can fathom all mysteries
and all knowledge, and if I have a faith that can move mountains
but do not have Love, I am nothing.
If I give all I possess to the poor and give over my body to hardship
that I may boast, but do not have Love, I gain nothing.
Love is patient, love is kind.
It does not envy; it does not boast. It is not proud.
It does not dishonor others. It is not self-seeking.
It is not easily angered. It keeps no records of wrongs.
Love does not delight in evil but rejoices with the Truth.
It always protects, always trusts, it always hopes, always perseveres.
Love never fails but where there are prophecies, they will cease.

Where there are tongues, they will be stilled.
Where there is knowledge, it will pass away.
For we know in part and we prophecy in part
but when completeness comes, what is in part, disappears.
When I was a child, I talked like a child,
I thought like a child, I reasoned like a child.
When I became a man, I put the ways of childhood behind me.
For now, we see only a reflection as in a mirror; then we shall see
face to face. Now I know in part, then I shall know fully
even as I am fully known. And now, these three remain.
Faith, Hope and Love but the greatest of these is Love.
—*1 Corinthians 13*

Today I am fortunate to be alive. I have a precious human life
and I am not going to waste it.
—*Dalai Lama XIV*

In the end, I realize that there are no endings. Each day is new. Each moment is a gift. I am learning to let go of judging other people and myself. I am learning to love and to let others live and wish them only well on their journeys.

I am learning to own my life and no one else's. No longer do I accept the imposition of the will of others to define me.

There is beauty and wonder all around us. The world is full of people we don't know and fascinating discoveries and true magic!

I started my journey in great pain and confusion. I believed in Santa. I once believed that orange was the best color to use for a skin tone in a schoolroom exercise. I believed that no one loved me and that no one ever would.

I invested the power of my belief into so many wrong things. For too much of my life, I believed those things.

I had issues with my family. All of those are gone. I have forgiven and asked forgiveness. I love them. I love you, Mom. I love you, Dad. Yes, I love you, Jeffy. I even learned that I can love me, as well. The time is so short that we get to share with those we love. I can't waste another minute on grudges. Yes, I still fall back into my limited fearful, selfish perspective. We are all a work in progress. I am learning to make better choices and create better beliefs.

I encourage you to learn to live that love. To do the hard things—asking forgiveness and forgiving—as well as finding the courage to face your fears. Our negative emotions have so much to teach us about how we mistreat and limit ourselves and others. Most of all, I encourage you to let go. Let go of master-debates within yourself and with other people. Instead, remember that both you and they are people who are traveling that same fearful, inhumane path.

What do you imagine would happen if we all started getting genuinely interested in why people believe what they believe, instead of comparing our beliefs to theirs in a struggle to be "right?" God knows that no one was ass-holey as I was when I was the king of moral judgments.

I simply can't blame other people for making the same mistake. I am no longer living from insanity, repeating the same cycles of imposing my will onto others or defining them in my image. I have begun the practice of only wishing them well. I know that they are in pain. They are lost in their limited perspectives, believing it to be reality, and I know that pain. I offer all of this to help people see clearly, as these realizations were given to me to share with you through my own pain.

I see now that pain isn't pointless. I now know that everything around me is a gift, which I can have as long as I don't resist it or run away. If I get curious, I can go through it and come out of it with a new understanding, a deeper look at the reality of this mystery. This is the way we grow. Every day, I realize more and more that life is a gift, happening for me and not to me. All suffering is a chance to learn.

A good friend told me something once. It's a famous quote from Ram Dass. I offer it to you now as an ending and a new beginning. "The reality is that we are all just walking each other home. We are all in this together."

Be kind to yourself and others. Use love as your guiding heart and the Golden Rule as your measure to end your master debates. See what you find, and I wish you only the best as we all walk each other home.

Acknowledgments

WRITING THIS BOOK HAS BEEN A JOURNEY. It has taken me seven years. I have written more than 3,000 pages and 10 versions of this book.

It has been a huge learning process that I didn't want to do in the beginning. There have been so many people who have helped me along the way, and they deserve recognition.

First and foremost, thank you, Mom and Dad. Dad, I learned so much from all your generosity and playfulness. Those are the best parts of me today. Mom, I always will love and appreciate our late nights watching musicals at the expense of school the next day.

I want to thank the teachers who gave me something worth way more than learning. To Jack Elias, I thank you for being the first to open my eyes to all of what I have discovered in writing this book. If you are curious about how to benefit from Jack's wisdom and expertise, you can find him at Finding True Magic, https://findingtruemagic.com.

I want to also thank Guy Finley for doing the same thing in a different way. His teachings are a true gift to me and whoever else is taking part. You can find him at Guy Finley.org.

As for people around me in daily life, I want to thank Rodney Nicklaw. You are a brother to me and a true friend. I couldn't have done this book without our conversations at the tea house.

Thank you, Christine and Big D (that means you, Danya) at the tea house, for always being kind and helpful while Rod and I drank our tea.

I want to thank Pat and Amanda Schmitter, who read some of those painful early drafts with all the football analogies in them. Pat, you adopted me when I first got here, and having you as my bonus mom and your reading aloud and pointing out my ridiculous overuse of commas made me realize that I am a true kamikaze.

Thank you to Earl Hurlburt, Scott Smith, Marcus Kim, Guru Daniel, and all the people I have met through the art of IOPS Silat. I would also like to thank my friends in the Forge, created by Marcus and Earl: Andy, David, Curt, and Larry.

I never experienced a martial art that is so complete and produces and encourages the best in people. You can find more about the art at Inti Ombak Pencak Silat, https://intiombak.com.

I have to thank my helpers, who made my life possible when I had my business and after I lost it due to the pandemic. That means you, Amanda Burlock, Amanda Green, and Amy Curtis. A special thank you goes out also to my helper Gail Sampson, who surprises me each week with new treasures and encouragements.

Thanks also to Mary Caron and her daughter Harmony. Mary, you are a wonderful gym partner and have saved me from so many injuries. I could not lift the ridiculous amounts of weight that I do without you.

I have to send out a special thank you to Simeon Geigel and the support that I received, and am still receiving, from the CVOEO Micro Business Development program here in Vermont, as well as the people at the Vermont Division for the Blind and Visually Impaired. The fact that so many people here treated me like a person who is blind, instead of a blind person, is the primary reason I stayed.

I also want to thank my amazing and talented cousins: Rachel, who did the cover art for the first edition of this book, and Christina. Your heart, strength, and career speak for themselves. Also my dearest Aunt Shelly. Your love and support and encouragement helped me to keep going when I doubted that I could find the key ingredients over the nine years that this project encompassed.

I don't forget you at all, Mike. Just because we aren't in touch much, you are in my heart and thoughts as a brother.

I definitely need to also send my true appreciation to Lisle Ann Jackson for introducing me to Jamie and Keith, as well as Mark Nisbett, who did much of the heavy lifting for the audio version and enhanced the new cover. Thank you for Fiona O'Brien's special gift of the inspiration of the new cover design and so much more, as well as the ENTIRE MBT community. You are all quickly becoming true friends, and your support and encouragement, as well as your kindness and humanity, have made me very grateful that I have found an online home.

We often don't realize how many people are helping us all along the way. A stranger who picked up and gave me my wallet when I unknowingly dropped it. Plenty of anonymous somebodies just holding the door to help me manage what I was carrying. Professionals who lent some of their time and expertise to help me figure out the process of writing a book after losing my sight. Thank you, Jen Hager. No one can write a book alone, without the help and contributions of other people; it's that way for everything in the world.

A very special thank you to Nichole Brigger, who ultimately formatted the first edition of this book. Apparently, the worst thing about it on submission was how it looked visually. Who knew?

A brand new cheer of thanks and appreciation to my editor, Louise Watson, who took this rough work and polished it into what it has become. I would not have been able to fully honor this project without her contributions. And thanks to Nancie Dunn, who introduced me to Louise. New thanks also to Steph at Gotham City Graphics for the internal layout and design of the book and the new electronic version.

Thank you to my good friend Pete Horner, who did the audio and helped along the way with long conversations, working out the confusion early in the process.

A thank you to those who beta read the book Bahzad Ballout and Michael Malarsie.

A thank you to my friends at the Unitarian Universalist Society, with special hugs for Scott and Pam—and to all my good friends, both known and as yet unknown.

Lastly, I want to thank my most favorite and beloved little person for always being there. Your ability to do so much and still find time for nightly s'mores has meant the world to me.

The world is built on a weave intertwining all of us. Look at all the good people in your life. From your most loved to the stranger you share a quick joke or kind word with on the street. There are so very many good people out there who are ready to be kind, be helpful, and share. People who make everything work and who can, in any moment, show a kindness and a humanity that makes this experience something more. A bit of sunlight breaking through the clouds. Look for them. Initiate the smiles and the kindnesses. Find small ways to surprise and delight each other. We are all in this together.

I also want to thank all of you who are reading this and sharing in our mutual journey. Take care of each other. Be kind.

About the Author

Steven Fidler was born and raised in southwestern Pennsylvania. He was part of a small family dynamic with one brother, a mom and dad, and a family dog. He expected to carve out a life like his father's...to make a decent living, buy a house, and create a small family of his own. Life had other plans, however. Steve ended up unexpectedly going blind and struggling with anxiety and depression, but ultimately realized, through a journey that he could never have imagined, that all of life is a gift.

He now lives with his favorite person in Vermont and explores the strange and amazing things that life has to offer—things like Reiki, martial arts, and a host of esoteric practices—seeking a deeper understanding of a world that is hiding in plain sight. You can often find him at the local tea house or at the Indian and Thai restaurants, enjoying good food and conversation with close friends and family.